Time-Fetishes

POST-CONTEMPORARY INTERVENTIONS

A Series Edited by Stanley Fish and Fredric Jameson

Titian, *Bacchus and Ariadne.*

National Gallery, London. Reproduced by permission

of Alinari/Art Resource, New York.

Time-Fetishes

The Secret History of Eternal Recurrence

Ned Lukacher

Duke University Press Durham and London

1998

Printed in the United States of America on acid-free paper ∞

Designed by C. H. Westmoreland

Typeset in Minion with Optima display by Tseng Information Systems, Inc.

Library of Congress Cataloging-in-Publication Data appear on the last

printed page of this book.

Das Alles wiederkehrt, ist die extremste Annäherung einer Welt
des Werdens an die des Seins: Gipfel der Betrachtung.

That everything recurs is the closest approximation of a world of
becoming to one of being: peak of the meditation.

FRIEDRICH NIETZSCHE

Der Fetisch bleibt das Zeichen des Triumphes
über die Kastrationsdrohung.

The fetish remains the sign of triumph over the threat of castration.

SIGMUND FREUD

Seulement l'objet de sa vision, ce qui le fit rire et trembler,
n'était pas le retour (et pas même le temps), mais ce que mit à nu le
retour, le fond impossible des choses.

Only the object of Nietzsche's vision, which made him laugh and tremble,
was not the return (and not even time), but what the return laid bare,
the impossible depth of things. GEORGES BATAILLE

Wie Ich den Ringschatten trage,
trägst du den Ring.

As I bear the Ring's shadow,
you bear the Ring.

PAUL CELAN

Contents

Preface and Acknowledgments

We cannot exist, we cannot live humanely except through the meanderings of time: the totality of time alone makes up and completes human life. How can we refer to this completed whole? GEORGES BATAILLE, *The Tears of Eros*

We die because we cannot connect the end to the beginning. ALCMAEON OF CROTON (fifth century B.C.)

In composing *Bacchus and Ariadne* (cf. the frontispiece to this book) Titian must have had in mind one of the most well known poems of the Roman poet Catullus (84–54 B.C.), poem 64, which describes how Bacchus and his entourage suddenly overtook Ariadne, who had just been abandoned by Theseus:

In another part the flowering Iacchus [Bacchus] was wandering
With a dance of Satyrs and Sileni from Nysa
Looking for you, Ariadne, and burning with love.
. . .
Some of the women shook long rods with covered points,
Some of them threw in the air the parts of a bull,
Some pulled round themselves a belt of twisted snakes,
Some thronged around the box which held the orgies,
The orgies which only initiates may be told of;
Others struck timbrels with palms uplifted
Or made slight tinklings with the polished brass:
Many blew horns and made a raucous noise
And barbarian pipes screamed out their horrible tunes.
(trans. C. H. Sisson)

As we will see in chapter 2, Titian was thinking of several literary depictions of this mythological scene. But consider Catullus's perspective, for whom the appearance of the god is synonymous with radical disruption, an anti-aesthetic din whose nerve center Catullus situates in the enigmatic "orgy box" (*orgia cistis*) around which the celebrants throng. Such caskets in fact contained the mysteries of the cult, its symbols and sacred objects, its secret language. The *ta orgia* of the ancient Greek Dionysian cults are, as Jean-Luc Nancy reminds us, not simply sexual objects but rather fetishes carefully inscribed within a ritual performance and calculated to produce the experience of "the propitious moment," the ecstatic *kairos* (*The Sense of the World*, 141–42). As we will see later, the cult's time-fetishes included a basket, a winnowing cloth, and the phallic *liknon*, which are choreographed through a kind of art, or *tekné*, in order to produce, as Nancy might say, the experience of "unbound time" (*temps déchainé*) (142), the experience of being liberated into a more authentic temporality, the time of a pure and absolute disruption of time's continuous and apparently endless flow, the kind of suspensive ritual disruption that Georges Bataille called "the sovereignty of the moment over utility" (*The Accursed Share*, vols. 2–3, 380).

I want to suggest in *Time-Fetishes* that the thought, idea, doctrine, or secret of eternal recurrence is very much, à la Catullus, the *ta orgia*, "the orgiastic things," of Western philosophy and literature, the secret "orgy box" to which only the initiates have access. It is not only the case, as Nancy has remarked, that "the thought of the eternal return is the inaugural thought of our contemporary history" (*Etre singulier pluriel*, 22); we can go further than that and say, and indeed demonstrate, that the thought of eternal recurrence is "the inaugural thought" in the effort by virtually every epoch to take the measure of time's unmeasurable otherness and mystery. Nietzsche's decision to become the teacher of eternal return signaled not only what Heidegger called "the completion of the history of metaphysics" but also the need for a reassessment of the role that eternal recurrence has played throughout that history. It is Nietzsche's teaching that is truly "inaugural" in Nancy's sense, insofar as it is both the last attempt at a systematic metaphysics that sought to account for the totality of existence and the "inaugural" attempt to think ironically about all metaphysical determinations in order better to prepare ourselves to affirm the abandonment and lack that truly characterize our historical relation to time and Being.

Because it is now apparent that the poetical-philosophical history of time and Being has concealed the fetish character of its keywords and concepts, it is important that we try to understand the relation of the *ta orgia* of the Greek and Roman bacchants to the discourses and images of Western thought quite literally and not at all analogically or metaphorically, for there are libidinal components, sadistic and erotic trends, clearly discernible within all prior determinations of the relation of time to Being. Thinkers and poets have invariably derived the nature of time from a prior determination of the meaning of Being, which has meant that the derivative character of the meaning of Being in relation to the enigma of time has generally been concealed and forgotten in Western metaphysics. Nietzsche's rediscovery of the ancient doctrine of return was at once the culmination and the reversal of a long history of secret desire and concealment. And that is why a "time-fetish" is not a critical sobriquet loosely based on a psychoanalytic analogy but rather the effort to name the fetish character of the languages of time in the West.

It was to this same scene of Bacchus's sudden discovery of Ariadne that Nietzsche turned in his poem "Ariadne's Lament," where in "a flash of lightning, Dionysus becomes visible in emerald beauty" and proclaims to Ariadne: "I am thy labyrinth" (*Dithyrambs of Dionysus*, 59). And the wisdom he proclaims is the same teaching we receive from Zarathustra, which is perhaps best summarized in this brief passage from "The Convalescent" in *Thus Spoke Zarathustra*. This is the labyrinth into which Bacchus would lead us:

Behold, we know what you teach: that all things recur eternally, and we ourselves too; and that we have already existed an eternal number of times, and all things with us. You teach that there is a great year of becoming, a monster of a great year [*ein grossem Jahre des Werdens, ein Ungeheuer von grossem Jahre*], which must, like an hourglass, turn over again and again so that it may run down and run out again; and all these years are alike in what is greatest as in what is smallest; and we ourselves are alike in every great year, in what is greatest as in what is smallest. (332)

As we will see repeatedly throughout *Time-Fetishes,* what is monstrous about the notion of the great year is its undecipherable labyrinthine character. There is no aesthetic or epistemological consolation in the cosmic vista of the universe as an eternally rotating hourglass but only the effect of disruption, of a break in the normative homogeneity of the time-stream. The circle or ring of sameness which time and the will appear to constitute in fact belie a monstrous labyrinth of infinite cycles in an unimaginable topology. The secret of the great year is one of the most precious of philosophy's *ta orgia.* Although the idea of eternal return readily betrays its fetish character, it also belies the monstrous non-knowledge which its figures and allegories can only hopelessly try to conceal. *Time-Fetishes* is concerned to locate material instances of the dynamic interplay of fetish prosthesis and monstrous lack in the discourses that try to articulate the relation of time and Being from the Presocratics to Nietzsche and beyond.

Shakespeare's role in the secret history of eternal recurrence is perhaps one of the more novel contentions of *Time-Fetishes.* Although he was not an advocate or disciple of the doctrine, his poetic understanding of the world was largely determined by Ovid's presentation of Pythagorean and Heraclitean versions of the doctrine. In several important respects, Shakespeare's stratagems in what he calls his "war with time" recall and repeat those of Ovid. Furthermore, Shakespeare's reinscription of Ovid's Heraclitean "river of time" follows all the diverse Ovidian tonalities, from the enlightened irony about desire and language in the Sonnets to the savage cruelties of the sexual will in virtually all of the plays. What could be more cruel, for example, than the monstrous mutilation of King Pentheus by his mother, Agave, and her bacchants when, in a trance of orgiastic passion, she beheads her son with her own hands, while her companions tear off his hands (*Metamorphoses* bk. 3, ll. 720–33)? I will return to the Dionysian elements underlying Shakespeare's accounts of the savage and ironic force of the will and what, like Georges Bataille, we might call an "acephalic" monstrosity at the heart of the moment's sovereignty; as though the acephalic body of time resembled nothing so much as a mutilated corpse. And yet, Ovid repeatedly proclaimed himself a disciple of Bacchus and dedicated his poetic vocation to the god. The sovereign or heterological disruption which the thought of eternal return brings into our everyday sense of time and world causes the world to tremble, to become unsteady, and yet also to reveal something of its essential nature. Shakespeare's "war with time" brings the irony and the savagery of the ancient world back to the forefront of European thought.

In my treatment of "The Ancients" I turn to some little known texts and images, above all to the role of Bacchus and Ariadne in the cult of Liber Pater, Libera, and Ceres, which flourished well into the late third century A.D. In an effort to set the iconographic context behind the literary imagery of Catullus, Ovid, or Plotinus, I turn to the sarcophagal art of the first and second centuries. What we will discover are the material remains of a culture and a cult that focused on the question of time and the possibility of eternal recurrence. This history still remains for the most part secret and long since buried by the success of Christianity in subduing all rival sects.

There are many other ancient images of circular or recurrent time, like the ouroboros, or serpent biting its own tail, which doubtless seemed to someone somewhere a perfectly serviceable image of time long before the first inscription of an Egyptian hieroglyph; or the image of the cosmic tree, which understandably fascinated Europeans as civilization spread further north and deeper into the forest. We will consider the Platonic and Neoplatonic genealogy of the well-known image of the Yggdrasill or "World Tree" in the Old Norse *Prose Edda* (c. 1200 A.D.), which, as it happens, also includes the serpentine figure of time's circularity.

In situating my readings of the philosophy of time, and of the poetic and iconographic imagery of eternity and eternal recurrence, my decisions were governed by a penchant for both the more highly figurative character of language and image and a concern to present what I thought were scenes that have generally gone unrecognized. Certain elements of *Time-Fetishes* will be elaborated and illuminated by a companion volume of readings that I call *Matter-Pieces: Toward a New History of Being*, which examines texts by St. Augustine, Shakespeare, Baudelaire, Bataille, and Blanchot. *Matter-Pieces* examines both the connection between the doctrine of return and the nature of poetic or literary language and the relation of my "secret history of eternal recurrence" to Heidegger's effort to decipher a more authentic "history of Being" beneath the now devalued and deconstructed history of Being as metaphysics. As Heidegger often remarks, what remained a secret throughout the history of Being as metaphysics was precisely the fact that it had forgotten *the question* of Being. *Time-Fetishes* is an account of those hitherto secret moments in the poetic-philosophical history of time in which the forgotten temporal horizon of the meaning of Being appears to be struggling toward some kind of recognition or iteration.

My selection of "Moderns" in *Time-Fetishes* is organized largely around the peculiarities of Nietzsche's articulation of the doctrine and thus seeks to trace pathways through which a characteristically Nietzschean dynamic of irony and a fetishizing aesthetic impulse works its way through the Marquis de Sade, Kant, Hegel, Schelling, and Schopenhauer before finding the way to Nietzsche, Trakl, Heidegger, Freud, and Derrida. Since the metaphysical determinations of the meaning of Being and the nature of time lie beyond the pale of logic and philosophy, it is tempting to regard the fictions of metaphysics as a literary ornament that can be easily shuffled off. But what is most significant about the "poetizing essence of reason," as Heidegger calls it, is that, although thinking and poetry both rely on it utterly, they do so in very different ways; for while poets often recognize the violence of their imposition of form upon the enigmatic stuff of time and Being, philosophers appear often not to recognize the poetic core of their thinking. There are, of course, exceptions and asymmetries that make this distinction nongeneralizable. Whether literary language is more alert and thus more ironic than philosophical language to the persistent dilemma of the aporia of time, or whether poets can be just as deluded and mesmerized by the time-fetish as the run-of-the-mill metaphysician, are among the many topics we will consider. If I had an overall goal in *Time-Fetishes,* it might be the effort to decipher the fundamentally ironic character of all the fetishized discursive and cultural formations that I treat. It is not for me to say whether I myself end up being captivated by the very fetishes I set out to expose, and whose rhetorical/aesthetic power, their illusion of transcendence,

I had meant to defuse. The general imperative that this book some-how tries to invoke might be something like "Build your time-fetishes ironically."

I would like to thank Richard Rand and Kerstin Behnke for invit-ing me to present portions of this work to audiences at, respectively, the University of Alabama and Northwestern University. I also want to thank the University of Illinois at Chicago for a very timely sab-batical leave during spring semester 1995. I am particularly grateful to Andrzej Warminski, Michael J. MacDonald, and Reynolds Smith for their detailed comments on an earlier version of this book, and to Philippa Berry, John Cullars, Jacques Derrida, Jay Geller, Brian Lu-kacher, Maryline Lukacher, J. Hillis Miller, and Susan Pezzino for their helpful remarks on aspects of this project.

I

The Ancients

Heraclitus maintained that the world was composed of fire, and that by
order of the destinies [*l'ordre des destinées*] must one day burst into
flame and consume itself; it would be reborn again one day. And of men
Apuleius said that they were "*Sigillatim mortales, cunctim perpetui,*"
"Individually mortal, eternal in their totality."

MICHEL DE MONTAIGNE

[Pythagoras] taught that the soul is immortal, and that after death
it transmigrates into other animated bodies. After certain specified
periods, he said, the same events occur again, for nothing is entirely new;
all animated beings are kin, he taught, and should be considered
one great family. Pythagoras was the first one to introduce
these teachings into Greece.

PORPHYRY

On such day as heaven's great year brings forth . . .

JOHN MILTON

The Anachrony of the Time-Fetish

The Pythagorean great year or Metakosmesis, to which Plato refers in *Timaeus* (37d) as the completion of the cosmological cycle wherein all astronomical bodies return to their original positions, was presumably, at least for Pythagoreans, a year of a calculable duration. It has turned out to be a very lengthy calculation indeed, and two and a half millennia later we are still waiting for the results. It is surely not the 38,000 years Plato may have supposed, and even today's cosmologists disagree by billions of years regarding the age and possible duration of the universe. Like the ancients, we moderns wonder if this model of a rotary astronomical cycle will be finally relevant to the configuration of the total cycle of the motion of our expanding universe. And if the total cycle does not take the form of a ring or circle, and if all that returns is an infinite nonreturn, then "the great year" might finally end up naming a most singular finitude, and the expiration of a limit that is really without anniversary or return, merely the measure of the lifespan or duration of a universe that repeats nothing and that can never be repeated. In view of such a narcissistically unappealing temporal horizon, which remains as unthinkable for many today as it has been throughout human history, is it any surprise that the meaning of time and eternity has always been prey to a certain predilection for time as a circular cycle? The very presupposition that the circle's anniversary or nuptial number existed in the first place and could be calculated lies at the foundation of all metaphysical determinations of the meaning of time and eternity.

Plato returned in the *Timaeus* not only to the great Pythagorean theme of the mystical number and the harmonies of universal motion but also to the accompanying theme of the finitude of the cosmos, which is to be distinguished from the emphasis of Ionian philosophy on the *apeiron,* the infinite, unbounded, or unconditioned from which the cosmos emerged. Plato, of course, addresses all these issues concerning the imposition and duration of limits, which culminate for him in the strange non-conceptual concept of the *khôra,* which is the maternal or nurselike receptacle or container for all the inorganic and organic matter in the cosmos (*Timaeus* 51b). The *Demiourgos* imprints the *paradigmea* on the matter within the *khôra.* The nature of the *khôra* and its neo-Platonic elaboration in the *Enneads* of Plotinus is a topic for later discussion. Here let us merely note that Plato alludes to its aporetic (*aporétatá*), perplexing or baffling, relation to thought and intelligibility. As we will see, *khôra* is a time-fetish, the fetish-name, if you prefer, for the enigmatic character of the question of time, for that which is neither becoming nor eternity and yet both of them at once. Aristotle will use the same language in *Physics,* book IV where he famously remarks that "time either does not exist at all or barely, and in an obscure way" (217b35). The aporia of time, in other words, is all about the difficulty that philosophy has always had in reappropriating the externality of time as universal motion in anything other than the subjectivist mode of a merely circular willing. And that is precisely why Aristotle decided to refocus the question of time, no longer on the impossible task of calculating the motion of the total cycle, what he calls "the cycling of the astronomical system" (*Physics* IV, 223b12), but on the "now time," the living present of the human subject. If the *khôra* names the threshold of the aporia of time, then the Aristotelian notion of durational time signals a decisive step back from the question of originary, nonsubjective time. While there is no access to the still withheld "true time" of the absolute cosmos, time is not simply durational time either. And yet these are the oppositions into which the philosophy of time has rigidly settled.

Rigorously speaking, we cannot say whether time is finite or infinite, or if there is an infinite series of finite universes that rise and fall, or whether creation is sequentially singular or simultaneously multiple (i.e., "the multiverse"). We can, however, consider what has been said, what arguments, concepts, words, and images have been used to indicate the persistent aporia of time and/or to conceal, evade, or simply ignore it. If one thinks one can calculate the great year, then one is playing a deluded astrological-theological game. But if one understands that the great year is only a marker, a formal notation of the still unthought essence of the meaning of time as the total cycle of the absolute cosmos, then the thought of the great year can, in effect, indicate the same aporetic impasse between our normal experience of time as continuous duration and time's enigmatic secret. *Metakosmesis* and *khôra* are at once time-fetishes, that is, names for time's impossible essence *and* names for the aporetic character of the time-question. It is this divided structure, or multiple nature, of the time-fetish that I want to adduce at the outset.

Because there is always an irreducible tonal instability, always a certain aporetic irony within every presumed principle of reason, when it comes to the words used to indicate the relation between the world of becoming and the realm of Being, between time and eternity, they are just as likely to be regarded as true concepts as they are poetic figures. They are most fetishlike when they appear as true descriptions of the world, as true accounts of what is living and what is dead; and that is because the fetish is precisely that which quickens the life of the subject by speeding up the circle of appropriation, by bringing the otherness of the other into the proximity of the self-same. But the interesting point about the time-fetish is that it combines this conventional fetish appeal with the absential or aporetic component; the time-fetish as fetish *and* antifetish, together, inseparable.

If metaphysical thinking, which takes so many forms (poetic, theological, architectural, etc.) may be said to be a kind of *Meta-Fetishismus* or "metafetishism," then my determination to read the secret history of the idea of eternal recurrence through a series of time-fetishes may be said to follow the effractions of what Freud regarded as a more subtle kind of fetishism, one characterized by a "divided attitude to castration" (*Standard Edition* 21:156). Not only is the castration of women both affirmed and denied, but such "subtle" fetishists are similarly divided in their attitude toward the castration of men. I adduce these Freudian reflections as analogous to the plurivocal stance of the time-fetish, which embraces the fetish and the aporia, and which is thus unlike the conventional fetish as ersatz or substitute for the noumenal thing-in-itself that merely disavows castration but never actively confronts the aporetic character of the time-question. The antinomical time-fetish tends, again in Freud's idiom, "to linger" over the question of time and thus over its aporia, while the traditional ontotheological metafetishist mistakes the sexual prosthesis as a pure substitute for the erogenous zones. Freud defined the perversions generally as a "lingering over [*Verweilungen*] the intermediate relations to the sexual object" and as an "extending beyond [*Überschreitungen*] the regions of the body that are designed for sexual union" (*SE* 7:150). To seek a certain satisfaction in the undecidability between the prosthesis and the castrated/uncastrated erogenous zone, rather than in the prosthesis itself, is perhaps not a bad description of what it means to read the secret history of eternal recurrence, where time's aporia has become the originary erogenous zone.

Freud provides the example of the "subtle" fetishist for whom a certain kind of athletic support-belt managed "to conceal the distinction between [male and female genitals]" (*SE* 21:157). This kind of fetish, "doubly derived from contrary ideas," holds particularly well (157). The antinomical spring that makes such a complex symptom essentially resistant to therapeutic modification adheres by virtue of joining fetishism, not simply to antifetishism, but to something other than fetishism. This sort of "divided attitude toward castration" seems to me to describe the antinomical structure of the temporal aporia between durational, subjective time and the cyclical motion of the entire system. In strictly Kantian fashion, time does and does not have a beginning, it is and is not finite and calculable. Although Kant might have preferred to speak of fetishism as a psychological paralogism rather than as a cosmological antinomy, the result is virtually the same. In Kant's idiom time-fetishes would be something like the theological ideals of pure reason, our minimally fetishistic phenomenalization of what is still a resistant noumenal absence. The difference between antinomies, paralogisms, and ideals ultimately lies, like Freud's symptoms, in their resistance to a resolution of their contradictions. We will consider Kant in more detail in chapter 5, so let me remark here only that Kant brings the epoch of Aristotelian durational time to a kind of closure, by making apparent the subjective presuppositions that had always ruled this regime of metaphysical phrases. Metafetishism is my Freudian rendering of Heidegger's critique of the history of Being as metaphysics, which has mangled the meaning of Being because it could not suspend its own will to power long enough to take account of the default or gap in Being, which is all that has actually ever appeared. Caught between a disavowal of castration and the hallucinated life of a prosthetic phallus, the metaphysical/metafetishist interpretation of time has always been derived from a prior determination of the meaning of Being. Metaphysics has always denied the temporal derivation of Being itself and in so doing has produced, not a philosophy of time, but a series of time-fetishes. If post-Kantian philosophy turns back to the question of time as precisely an antinomical double aporia, and if this is the great legacy of Kant for Hegel, Schopenhauer, and Nietzsche, then what might the (ironic) history of the time-fetish look like? What makes this an ironic history is that it tends to reveal an opposition between the crude (or less subtle) fetishism of the dominant metaphysical tradition and the subtle fetishism at work in the secret history of pagan and modern fetishes with their doctrine of eternal recurrence.

When Nietzsche looked back in *Ecce Homo* for historical precedents of his own version of the doctrine, he focused on Heraclitus:

I have looked in vain for signs of it even among the *great* Greeks in philosophy, those of the two centuries before Socrates. I retained some doubt in the case of *Heraclitus*, in whose proximity I feel altogether warmer and better than anywhere else. The affirmation of passing away *and destroying*, which is the decisive feature of a Dionysian philosophy; saying Yes to opposition and war; *becoming*, along with a radical repudiation of the very concept of *being*—all this is clearly more closely related to me than anything else thought to date. The doctrine of the "eternal recurrence," that is, of the unconditional and infinitely repeated cyclical course of all things [*Kreislauf*]—this doctrine of Zarathustra *might* in the end have been taught already by Heraclitus. At least the Stoa has traces of it, and the Stoics inherited almost all of their principal notions from Heraclitus. (*Ecce Homo* 272–74, translation modified)

The self-proclaimed "last disciple of the philosopher Dionysus" (*Twilight of the Idols*, 563) is more properly speaking Heraclitus's last disciple, and one who is indebted as well to the Heraclitean Stoics with their emphasis, not on the great year but on the completion of the world-cycle as world-conflagration or *ekpyrosis*. In this connection, Nietzsche is surely thinking of Heraclitus's fragment 37: "This cosmos, the same for all, was made by neither a god nor a man; but it always has been and will be fire ever-living, kindling itself in measures, and quenching itself in measures" (trans. McKirahan, in *Philosophy before Socrates*, 124). The phrase "fire ever-living" (*pyr àeízöon*) takes us directly to the central issue from which we will never stray very far or for very long: the question of the temporal relation between the living being and the fiery, ever rising and falling, river of time, here instanced by the linkage between fire, life, *zoé*, and eternity, *aei*. The measures or *métra* are presumably identical with what fragment 43a, an apocryphal fragment, calls "the great year," or *praeterea annus* (the only version of this fragment is in Latin), which culminates in *ekpyrosis* (the only Greek word in this fragment): "This cycle consists of 10,800 years" (Kahn, *Art and Thought of Heraclitus*, 49). Here we see in brief how Heraclitean *ekpyrosis* became assimilated to the Pythagorean great year. For Nietzsche the destructive, Dionysian, aspect of the eternal cycle was precisely what remained most essential about the doctrine.

Nietzsche also admired Heraclitus's understanding of just this relation between life and eternity, particularly as it appears in fragment 52: "*Aion* is a child playing checkers." The word *aion* is the key to the problem here. *Aion, eón, aei:* do these words mean eternal duration, an eternal present, or an individual lifespan, the time of the world or the time of a living being? The meanings of this word sketch out the history of the subjectivization of the meaning of time; which is what Heidegger meant when he said, in his reading of Anaximander, that "the fate of the West hangs on the translation of the word *eón*" ("The Anaximander Fragment," 33). This may seem a portentous utterance, but it conveys, I believe, a central and important insight. Let us see how two translations of Heraclitus's saying reveal precisely this confusion between *aion* as the individual lifespan, that is, subjective duration, and *aion* as world-time, that is, the total cosmic cycle.

Charles Kahn chose the former (Kahn, *Art and Thought of Heraclitus*, 71), while John Sallis and Kenneth Maly picked the latter (Sallis and Maly, *Heraclitean Fragments*, 11). The plurivocality of the saying of the meaning of presence, and above all its irreducible division, remains, it would appear, unsayable even today. Are we ready to listen to Heraclitus and hear what he has to say about *aion*?

Let us begin with Nietzsche's sense of fragment 52. Nietzsche understood *aion* in Heraclitus as naming the duration of "the impermanence of everything actual, which constantly acts and comes-to-be but never is" (*Philosophy in the Tragic Age of the Greeks*, 54). Nietzsche wanted, of course, to recover a primordial sense of the word that had been lost by repeated renderings into the register of eternity, permanence, and Being. Nietzsche concludes with his central observation: "Heraclitus as a human being was unbelievable. Even if he were observing the games of noisy children, what he was thinking was surely what no other man had thought on such an occasion. He was thinking of the great world-child Zeus" (67). Nietzsche's Heraclitus reopens the question of time's relation to Being. But he unnerves us as he deprives us of any principle of certainty by comparing the emergence of the cosmos to the caprice of child's play. Only by risking everything on chance does the "ever-living fire" achieve an eternally recurrent presence.

In a remarkable and indispensable essay entitled "Le sens philosophique du mot *Aion*," A. J. Festugière has traced a bizarre philological history in which the meanings of *aion* and *chronos* are effectively reversed or exchanged in the centuries between Homer and Aristotle. *Aion*, which originally meant an individual lifespan, becomes an abstract eternal living present, and *chronos*, which had meant absolute time, the duration of the astronomical cycle, comes to mean the calculation of duration in the world of becoming. In the *Timaeus*, for example, Plato regarded *aion* as the eternal present or "ever being" (*aei einai*), the unchanging form or model in the realm of intelligibility. Time as *chronos*, as measurable duration, becomes, famously, "the moving image of eternity" (*aionis eikon*). *Chronos* became mere copy, the cyclical recurrence of *aion*. Nietzsche's reading of *aion* in his early lectures on *Philosophy in the Tragic Age of the Greeks* reveals that

Plato's abstraction of *aion* from the world of becoming had already lost the fundamental sense of the Heraclitean saying, which was that the ever-living fire of time and becoming lives its life and dies its death like a living being. The antinomy of this paradox is that the ever-living survives by dying, by suspending itself. Zeus as the god who survives *ekpyrosis* is a well-known Stoic allegory, and Montaigne speaks of the belief of Chrysippus "that all gods died in the last conflagration of the world, except for Jupiter. . . . Diogenes of Apollonia says God is Time" ("Apology for Raymond Seybond," *Complete Essays,* trans. Screech, 575). Nietzsche's favorite name for the god who survives, for the god who recurs eternally, was not, of course, Zeus but Dionysus, who literally underwent gestation within, and was delivered from, his father's, Zeus's, body. The significant point is surely that for Nietzsche Heraclitean *aion* names that specifically Dionysian experience of time and becoming to which Nietzsche devoted most of his later years.

Aion itself appears to name the site or topos where something like what Heidegger calls the forgetting of the ontological difference between beings and Being may actually have occurred. If time/eternity is like a divine child, and if the world is like a game it plays, then, for all the differences between gods and mortals, there remains a strange likeness and sameness. *Aion* thus comes to name both the inaccessible otherness of time and its everydayness and immediacy in the world of becoming. Plato, as we will see, struggled against the spell of Parmenidean Being and against the temptation to disengage *aion* from the enigma of the truth of time. The *tertium quid* of Plato's *khôra*, neither myth nor logic, takes us back to the crisis of determining the past and future of spatial extension. The Heraclitean saying and Nietzsche's reading indicate that we are concerned with not only a resistant, anomalous time-kernel that cannot be reduced to becoming or to eternity, but also with the even stranger mystery of an undecidable relation between the time of human existence and the time of Being.

It is important to understand that the doctrine of eternal recurrence is not simply a matter for philosophy as it struggles to emerge from mythic thinking, but that it also has significant connections to the ancient mystery cults. Following the leitmotifs of Nietzsche's effort to revive the doctrine of eternal recurrence, I want to suggest that we bring

together Nietzsche's learned intuition that eternal return was the esoteric secret of the cults and the work of Walter Burkert and Albert
Henrichs on archaic Greek religion. While Nietzsche emphasized the
desire of the human will to see itself as something eternal, historians
of the cults have been reluctant to acknowledge a role in the cults for
rebirth or resurrection. Burkert, for example, is wary of linking the
mysteries to these ideas: "Nor should they be used as the exclusive key
to the procedures and ideology of mysteries" (*Ancient Mystery Cults*,
101). In the characteristic Dionysian ritual, the priestess (and only
married women were admitted to these rites, Burkert insists) would
unveil the *liknon* or phallic fetish that was carried in a winnowing basket and covered by a cloth. Burkert ironizes the scene of unveiling,
which he suggests was performed "with laughter in a playful mood,"
indicating that it "was hardly the core of the mystery" (105). We might
take a step beyond Burkert's somewhat excessive skepticism, which
holds both that the doctrine of return might not be the key to the
mysteries and that the ritual revelation of the *liknon* was a somewhat
frivolous or parodic affair. Here Nietzsche is, I believe, more helpful
for having grasped the more essential fact that it is precisely the fusion
of the mock-sexual ritual with an esoteric doctrine about time and
existence itself that made the cult of Bacchus/Liber Pater such a long-
standing theory and practice.

Let us turn here not to the historians of ancient religion but to
Nietzsche, who thought that what lay at the core of the cults was the
idea of "eternal life, the eternal recurrence of life [*die ewige Wiederkehr des Lebens*], the promise and the consecration of procreation,
the triumphal affirmation of a life beyond death [*Leben über Tod*],
the *true* life as the going forth together in community, in the city,
in the relation between the sexes" (*Kritische Studienausgabe* 13:628).
This notebook entry from spring 1888 simply restates precisely what
Nietzsche's version of the doctrine had always been about. A certain
"fecundity" with respect to life was always the focus: "Life itself, its
eternal fecundity and recurrence [*Fruchtbarkeit und Wiederkehr*] determine the torment, the destruction, the will to annihilation" (*KSA*
13:266). Although no philosopher of the nineteenth century was more
alert than Nietzsche to the accidental nature of human evolution, and

no thinker confronted the implications of Darwinian theory more directly or more powerfully than he, his version of the doctrine would nevertheless emphasize the resilience of life. As he remarked in *The Gay Science*, "the formation of the organic [is] an exception of exceptions" (§ 109). Modern eternal recurrence is not an imitation of the ancient doctrine but its reactivation in a modern context. It was in 1883 that Nietzsche claimed to have uncovered the secret of the Greek mysteries: "they believed in eternal recurrence: that is the mystery-belief" (*KSA* 10:340). He had decided in August 1881 to see if he could actually will himself into believing in eternal recurrence, into reactivating the ancient will to see oneself as eternal. The gist of this notebook entry is: "the ancients could believe it, why can't I?"

As a matter of writing and language, this meant rediscovering the fundamental sense of *aion* as "force of life, source of vitality" (Benveniste, cited by Festugière, 270), of time as infinitely regenerating duration. Back again to his lectures from 1869, Nietzsche contrasts Heraclitus's sense of an oscillating universe with the finally very similar ideas of Schopenhauer, which differ, however, in "the basic tone of their description," for while Heraclitus affirms his rising-falling river of fire, Schopenhauer cannot affirm such strife and sees it only as "proof of the internal self-dissociation of the Will to Live, which is seen as a self-consuming, menacing and gloomy drive, a thoroughly frightful and by no means blessed phenomenon" (*Philosophy in the Tragic Age of the Greeks*, 56). The passage continues in its description of Heraclitean ekpyrotic world-regeneration: "The arena and object of the struggle is matter, which the natural forces alternately try to snatch from one another, as well as space and time whose union by means of causality is this very matter." Against Schopenhauer's ascetic contempt for "the internal self-dissociation of the Will to Live," and against his hope for a nirvanic-buddhistic cessation of all world-cycles, Nietzsche marshals the counterdiscourses of eternal return.

Heraclitus, wrote Nietzsche, "raised the curtain on this greatest of all dramas": "What he saw, the teaching of *law in becoming* and of *play in necessity*, must be seen from now on in all eternity" (68). The thought of eternal recurrence as the law of universal impermanence and endless coming-to-be is, however, "a terrible, paralyzing thought" (54). Nietzsche's return to Heraclitus and to the ancient mystery cults was an effort to inaugurate a new beginning. It was Parmenides, of course, whom Nietzsche called "the counter-image" of Heraclitus: "likewise expressing a type of truth-teller but one formed of ice rather than fire, pouring cold piercing light all around" (69). The Parmenidean refusal of Heraclitean eternal becoming is for Nietzsche the great disaster of Western philosophy. This is the primal scene of the oblivion of the Being-question, for in "deriv[ing] absolute being from a forever subjective concept" (83) Parmenides severed the meaning of *eón/aion* from the temporal horizon of Being. In fragment 8, for example, we read: "Being is close to Being. But it is motionless in the limits of mighty bonds, without beginning [*anarchon*], without cease [*apauston*], since Becoming and Destruction have been driven very far away, and true conviction has rejected them" (line 5, trans. Freeman, *Ancilla*). Michael Theunissen reads Parmenides in precisely Nietzsche's sense when he writes: "The intrinsic not-being of Being manifests itself as not-living. Being, which also does not exist insofar as it is neither the world in its diversity nor God in his fullness, sinks into the nothingness of death; its perfection is the stillness of paralysis. At least in its initial form, metaphysics was actually what Nietzsche makes it out to be: nihilism" (Theunissen, "Metaphysics' Forgetfulness of Time," 23). Parmenides wanted to liberate thinking from the burden of time and life: "Presumably," writes Theunissen, "it is suffering from life that induced the Eleatic to formulate his concept of Being" (25). And radical purity from all contamination from the world of becoming could only be secured by situating the *tó on*, or Being, in a timeless present, *aéi*, eternally existing, and precisely no longer living. "Because all becoming is extinguished," writes Theunissen, "no one need fear that even a kernel of life will ever bestir itself again" (19). The great Parmenidean theme of the sameness that is shared by thinking and Being may perhaps be most notable for its anti-Heraclitean circumvention of the aporia of time, and for its turn from a subtle to a more elementary fetishism.

If Parmenides disavowed the paralyzing Heraclitean vision of eternal return and erected the fetish-idea of an autonomous self-subsisting realm of thought, it was Anaximander who anticipated the moral interpretation of the meaning of Being. Nietzsche's Anaximander asks: "Even now fire is destroying your world; some day it will go up in fumes and smoke. But ever and anew, another such world of ephemerality will construct itself. Who is there that could redeem you from the curse of coming-to-be?" (*Philosophy in the Tragic Age of the Greeks*, 48). Anaximander asked the question: "Whence the ever-renewed stream of coming-to-be?" but his answer, according to Nietzsche, was a "mystic" evasion: "Eternal coming-to-be can have its origin only in eternal being; the conditions for the fall from being to coming-to-be in injustice are forever the same; the constellation of things is such that no end can be envisaged for the emergence of individual creatures from the womb of the 'indefinite.' Here Anaximander stopped, which means he remained in the deep shadows which lie like gigantic ghosts upon the mountains of this world view" (50). Nietzsche's Anaximander seems to have confronted the aporia of time and then to have "fled into the womb of the metaphysical 'indefinite' [*apeiron*] to escape the definite qualities" (58). And this was why he tried to provide a moral rationalization as a way of standing back from the abyss of infinite time that opened around him. And this may also be why, as Nietzsche remarked in his lectures at Basel in 1875, Anaximander interpreted "natural extinction and generation morally in terms of guilt and punishment" (*Philosophy and Truth*, 135). Within the necessity of "use" or *tó chreón*, the usage of things, within, in other words, the cycles of recurrence, Anaximander envisioned a principle of justice or *diké* through, precisely, "the assessments of time" (*ton tou chronon taxis*).

Here is part of the so-called Anaximander fragment: "And the source of coming-to-be for existing things is that into which destruction, too, happens according to necessity [*kata tó chreón*]; for they pay penalty and retribution to each other for their injustice [*adikia*] according to the assessments of time" (Kirk and Raven, *The Presocratic Philosophers*, 106). Like Empedocles, Anaximander thinks of the absolute time of the total cosmological system as the unconditioned *apeiron ainos*, which, like the *aperas aion* of Empedocles (fragment 8), we might render, not as "boundless eternity," but as "illimitable duration." In another version of the fragment Anaximander is said to have "declared that destruction, and much earlier coming-to-be, happen from infinite ages [*apeiron ainos*], since they are all occurring in cycles" (*Presocratic Philosophers*, 107). Perhaps Charles Mugler has come closest to Anaximander's sense of the world when he observes that Anaximander's albeit very sketchy cosmology may have influenced the way that Greek tragedy "makes its characters accept death and destruction. . . . Such was the opinion of Nietzsche, who sought, as one inspired by the example of the Greeks, to revive the tragic conscience of contemporary Europe by reinventing Anaximander's doctrine of eternal recurrence" (Mugler, *Devenir cyclique,* 23). If Mugler is right about the cultural sense of Anaximander's saying, that it affirms or accepts the necessity that apportions justice and injustice through the distribution of "coming-to-be" (or the world of becoming) and the intervals of destruction that regulate the cycles, then this may well be precisely the ancient sense of recurrence that Nietzsche sought to reactivate.

This very question is Heidegger's focus in his essay entitled "The Anaximander Fragment," where he says that, although the history of metaphysics began with Anaximander and ended with Nietzsche's thought of eternal return, there are nevertheless important differences between these two ways of "bring[ing] the Same to language" ("The Anaximander Fragment," 23). Heidegger's objective is to rethink Anaximander, and to retranslate him, in terms that no longer bear any juridical-moral import. Although the development and complexity of Heidegger's response to Nietzschean eternal recurrence will occupy our attention in chapter 7, it is important to note here that Heidegger treats Anaximander's saying as something like the original blueprint of eternal return in the history of philosophy, the complexity of which has never been fully recognized. Here, as throughout Heidegger's work, the task of reading is to allow the words (in this case, Anaximander's) to "achieve their active nature by losing [*verlieren*] those qualities with which metaphysics has endowed them" (*Identity and Difference*, 37). Heidegger avoids the anthropocentric-moral reading by rendering *dike/adikia,* not as justice/injustice, but as jointure/disjunction. Heidegger's Hamletian turn of phrase for the Anaximanderian big bang / big crunch as "out of joint," *aus den Fugen,* means that "the assessments of time" have nothing to do with

any human notion of justice but merely state the disjointedness with
which the world of becoming comes to presence from out of the unconditioned *apeiron:* "The fragment says: what is present as such,
being what it is, is out of joint" ("The Anaximander Fragment," 41).
While Anaximander's phrase *didonai dike* is usually translated as "giving justice," Heidegger suggests that this really means the giving of
limits, *peras,* the conditioning of the unconditioned: "the sending
of boundaries of the while to whatever lingers awhile in presence"
(54). Presence, that is, "whatever lingers," would be distinct from the
present, which is thus sent or joined to presence in the act of this
giving. The "assessments" are not judgments but a joining and disjoin-
ing of presence to the present: "What belongs to that which is present
is the jointure of its while, which it articulates in its approach and
withdrawal" (43).

The still enigmatic heart of this giving and of this gift is indicated
only by the phrase *tó Chreón,* which for Heidegger names "the still
hidden essence of the gathering which clears and shelters." "What
is thought as *chreón* in the fragment is the first and most thoughtful interpretation of what the Greeks experienced in the name *Moira*
as the dispensing of portions [*das Erteilen des Anteils*]. *Tó Chreón,*
usage [*der Brauch*] is the handing over [*das einhandigende Aushandi-
gen*] of what is in each case present into its while in unconcealment"
(55). What Heidegger finds most interesting about Anaximander is
that this handing over, this dispensation of usage, is a kind of essential
disorder that in effect "conjoins the dis-" (*Der Brauch fügt da Un-*),
and worlds a world only by virtue of this ability to send itself "out
of joint." And it is perhaps in this sense that Heidegger could most
agree with Nietzsche that Anaximander remains, vis-à-vis the question of time, in the ghostly shadows of mountaintops, looming unseen
and inaccessible. Indeed, this is exactly how Heidegger characterizes
Nietzsche's thought of return, as placing Nietzsche himself in the same
shadowy impasse in which Nietzsche had last glimpsed Anaximander:
"wrapped in dark clouds. . . . The reasons do not lie in any inability in
Nietzsche, although his various attempts to demonstrate that the eternal recurrence of the same was the Being of all becoming led him curiously astray. It is the matter itself which is named by the term 'the eter-

nal return of the same' that is wrapped in a darkness from which even
Nietzsche had to shrink back in terror" (*What Is Called Thinking?* 108).

Is there really, however, a way through or around the darkness
named by *tó chreón* or eternal return? Heidegger seems to think so,
or at least he wants to believe that he might escape the judgments
of time that have overtaken his predecessors: "The darkness of this
last thought of Western metaphysics must not mislead us, must not
prompt us to avoid it by subterfuge [*Ansflüchte*]." Perhaps thinking
itself must inevitably turn to subterfuge when confronted with the
aporia of time, with the (dis)junction of *peras* and *apeiron*. And might
not that be because "usage," "need," or "necessity" are only finally
very inappropriate names for a temporal enigma, which is whether or
not time is a singular event that moves through a singular topology?
Like Nietzsche's doctrine and the Heraclitean ever-living fire, they are
only fetishlike names for a configuration of time and eternity, becoming and Being, for which we do not yet have a concept.

Commenting on Heidegger's "The Anaximander Fragment," Der-
rida recognizes in the *adikia*, in the *Un-Fuge,* the disjointure, the order
of "incoercible différance": "This element itself is neither living nor
dead, present nor absent: it spectralizes. It does not belong to ontology, to the discourse on the Being of beings, or to the essence of
life or death" (*Spectres of Marx,* 51). Derrida calls the experience of the
aporia of time — the impossibility and the necessity of trying to think
about the meaning of true time — a "sort of non-contemporaneity of
the present with itself," a "radical untimeliness" or "anachrony," an
anomalous temporality that is the disjointure of the present between
the going by of what was and the arrival of what is coming (*Spectres
of Marx,* 25). The task of thinking the irreducibility of anachrony, of
the necessity that it be named, and of the impossibility (at least for
now) of knowing the referent of that name become for Derrida synonymous with thinking the meaning of justice: "Does not justice as
relation to the other suppose . . . the irreducible excess of a disjointure or an anachrony, some *Un-Fuge,* some 'out of joint' dislocation
in Being and in time itself, a disjointure that, in always risking evil,
expropriation, and injustice (*adikia*) against which there is no calculable insurance, would alone be able to *do justice* or *to render justice* to

the other as other?" (27). The first step toward reversing philosophy's foreclosure of the other is to think the otherness of time.

It is this double structure of anachrony that I call a time-fetish, which both affirms the aporia of time and yet insists, inevitably and irresistibly, on giving its hidden essence a necessarily improper name. As Derrida has recently remarked, the doubleness of this anachronic disjointure defines an immense topic in the history of philosophy. He contends that philosophy from Plato to Heidegger is "an anti-time or *contretemps*—an effort to compensate and thus to resist the originary loss of this other time, of this time before time, and thus to aim for the restitution of the loss. . . . The *contretemps* of philosophy would thus come as a *contretemps* to resist this other *contretemps* that will have been the absolute time of the untenable promise" ("Avances," 30). There have always been two "countertimes": the resistant, aporetic character of true (or absolute) time, and philosophy's attempt to pass off its prosthetic replacement for the thing-in-itself. This is the same structure we spoke of earlier in regard to philosophy as crude metafetishism and as subtle, antinomical fetishism. All of philosophy's efforts to think true time as a circle were actually counterefforts against naming time's otherness as otherness and not as self-sameness, not in terms of a human subject's surmise about presence and duration. The subtle postmetaphysical fetishist desires neither true time nor the prosthesis but the undecidable suspension between them, the "incoercible différance" between two countertimes.

Consider once again the place of Parmenides in this speculative history of the double bind of the time-fetish. Is he not the pre-Socratic who tightened the bond of the rude fetish so tightly that it has resisted for millennia any effort to expose the two sides of the time question? "Nor will the force of true belief [*pistis*] allow," says Parmenides, "that, beside what is, there could also arise anything from what is not; wherefore Justice [*Dike*] looseth not her fetters to allow it to come into being or perish, but which holdeth fast; and the decision on these matters rests here: it *is* or it is not" (Kirk and Raven, *Presocratic Philosophers*, 273). Parmenides envisioned a powerful "avenging *Dike* [who] controls the double bolts [to the gates of the ways of Night and Day]" (*Presocratic Philosophers*, 267). Parmenides secured Being from nonbeing by separating it off from the question of time. At the opposite extreme, Heidegger regarded Nietzsche's doctrine of recurrence as similarly bypassing the aporia of time by eternalizing the world of becoming itself: "The will that is eternal in this sense no longer follows and depends on the temporal in what it wills, or in its willing. It is independent of time. And so can no longer be affronted by time" (*What Is Called Thinking?* 98). We might regard the time-fetish as naming the historical event of confronting and concealing the anachronic structure of the time question. Heidegger can make such an argument, however, only by ignoring the tonality of Nietzsche's writing, its irony and its paradoxes.

Here is Parmenides again: "There is not a Being which existed only during some past time, or will exist only in some future time, because at the present all Being is in being, together with itself, in one single continuum" (Parmenides, fragment 8.5, trans. Herman Frankel, "Studies in Parmenides," 46). While Parmenides elided anachrony when he removed Being from the aporia of past and future, Heidegger's Nietzsche erred at the other extreme by concealing the aporia of time behind an ironic metaphysical affirmation of eternal becoming. "All that is left [in Nietzsche]," writes Heidegger, "is the single surface [*ein einzige Fläche*] of a 'life' that empowers itself to itself for its own sake" (*Nietzsche III*, trans. Krell, 176 [slightly modified]). Together, Parmenides's single continuum of Being and Nietzsche's single surface of becoming define the most extreme historical configurations in which the time-fetish sought to conceal anachrony.

The loosening of the Parmenidean knot began at least as early as Plato's *The Sophist* with its idea of a hybrid kind of Being, the Being of nonbeing / the nonbeing of Being, a *triton genos* or third modality of Being that Plato calls an "intertwining" or *symplöke* (*Sophist* 240c). Such anomalous states of Being mark the limits of knowledge and keep a space open for the unthought. While the genealogy of Parmenidean Being leads through Aristotle's notion of the "prime mover" as "thought thinking itself" (*noesis noeseos*) (*Metaphysics* 1074b34) and dominates much of the spiritual history of the West, the Heraclitean-Anaximanderian genealogy of the names for time's namelessness, in other words, the genealogy of eternal recurrence, would constitute a kind of counterhistory, a strange kind of "bastard reasoning," as Plato

calls it in the *Timaeus*, neither *muthos* nor *logos*. This is what Plato
says about the *khôra touton*, the receptacle of all becoming (49b):
"A third kind [*triton genos*] is ever-existing Place [*khôras*] which ad-
mits not of destruction, and provides room for all things that have
birth, itself being apprehensible by a kind of bastard reasoning by
the aid of non-sensation, barely an object of belief" (52b); "of a kind
that is invisible and unshaped [*amorphon*], all-receptive, and in some
most perplexing and most baffling way [*aporétatá*] partaking of the
intelligible" (51b). Since it "belongs to neither sensory being nor to
intelligible being," writes Derrida, "neither to becoming nor to eternity, the discourse on *khôra* is no longer a discourse on being, it is
neither true nor probable and appears thus to be heterogeneous to
myth" ("Khôra," 113). The *khôra*, as an eternally existing possibility of
coming-to-presence, lies at the limits of philosophy as a kind of ex-
perimental speculation. "Not having an essence," Derrida continues,
"how could the *khôra* be beyond its name? The *khôra* is anachronistic;
it 'is' the anachrony within being, or better: the anachrony of being"
("Khôra," 126). The time-fetish names the aporia that lies beyond the
name. The impossibility of being beyond the name is what Heidegger means when he speaks of "being bound to the mother tongue,"
"bound to language and to the experience of its essence" ("The Anaximander Fragment," 19). What Plato calls "the Mother and Receptacle of this generated world" (51a) is, as Derrida remarks, "a strange
mother who gives place without engendering" (*On the Name*, 124).
More like a nurse than a mother, she/it marks the vanishing point of
Plato's thinking about the (dis-)jointure of the enigmatic difference
between Being and the aporetic horizon of unreadable time. Plato's
khôra seems to imply that the *metéra kai hypodoche* (mother and receptacle) of all that comes to presence is very much like a living being,
who somehow survives the great year.

Heidegger observed early in his lectures on Nietzsche in 1937 that
the doctrine of eternal recurrence "thinks nothing else than the
thought that pervades [*durcherrscht*] the whole of Western philosophy, a thought that remains concealed [*verhüllt*] but is its genuine
driving force [*der eigentlich treibende*]. Nietzsche thinks the thought
in such a way that in his metaphysics he reverts [*zurückkommt*] to the

beginnings of Western philosophy" (*Nietzsche* I, trans. Krell, 19). It is interesting, therefore, that Heidegger did not inquire into the aporetic temporal character of *khôra* but instead took a decidedly Parmenidean slant on its interpretation and related it to the *khorismos* or gap between Being and beings. In other words, instead of reading the strong indications in Plato that *khôra* is a material entity that lives eternally between Being and becoming, Heidegger de-realizes it as an existent being and reinvents it as a mere gap or notational spacing or interval:

> An interpretation decisive for Western thought is that given by Plato. He says that between beings and Being there prevails the *khôrismos; é khôra* is the *locus,* the site, the place. Plato means to say: beings and Being are in different places. Particular beings and Being are differently located. Thus when Plato gives thought to the different location of beings and Being, he is asking for the totally different place of Being, as against the place of beings.
>
> To make the question of the *khôrismos,* the *difference* in placement of beings and Being at all possible, the *distinction*—the duality of the two— must be given beforehand in such a way that this duality itself does not as such receive specific attention. (*What Is Called Thinking?* 227).

Heidegger's natural tendency as a thinker runs so powerfully in the Parmenidean direction of thinking, not toward the interminable impurity of the difference, which is Nietzsche's obsession, but toward the purity and noncontamination of the duality of beings and Being, of their "totally different" sites. Heidegger thus missed a great opportunity to link *khôra* to the secret history of eternal recurrence, that is, to the secret history of names and discourses that think the possibility of an unthought relation between time, eternity, and the living.

When Nietzsche remarked in his notes that "the doctrine of return is the *turning*-point [*Wende*-punkt] of history" (*KSA* 10:515), he was probably thinking of his own role as the new purveyor of a very ancient idea. As Nietzsche knew very well, there have been many important turning points in that history. Plato's notion of an "ever-existing Place" (*Khôras aeí*) still bears the Heraclitean, Pythagorean resonance of the "ever-living Place" and constitutes, I have argued, a step away from Parmenidean purity and toward Heraclitean becoming. It was, however, a step whose provisional and, as Plato puts it, "merely verbal" status (51c) has ensured it a marginal place in the history of philosophy. While Derrida has finally inscribed *khôra* in the counter-history of the *contretemps,* I want to consider a chapter in that history that has thus far gone entirely unnoticed. It is once again a matter of the interpretation of the meaning of *khôra,* more precisely of Plotinus's interpretation of *khôra* as *Khôragus,* which becomes the name, not only for the totality of becoming, but for the total structure containing all the modalities of Being and becoming. Plotinus asks us to imagine the universe in its entirety in the exceptionally singular image of an unimaginably immense theatrical production. What makes this moment so significant, however, is that Plotinus, who flourished in the middle of the third century A.D., was also the last major thinker of eternal recurrence in the West until, as I will argue in chapter 3, Shakespeare embarked on his reinvention of the Heraclitean cosmology of Ovid's *Metamorphoses* in the last years of the sixteenth century. Plotinus was also the last important thinker of eternal return arising from ancient Greek philosophy, and thus, even though he chronologically follows Ovid and the late Roman Bacchic cults I will consider in chapter 2, Plotinus's thinking remains closer to Plato than to the religious symbolism of eternal return that was widespread in the Roman world he actually inhabited.

As far as I have been able to determine, Richard Sorabji is perhaps the only student of this period in the history of philosophy who has noticed that Plotinus was a thinker of eternal return: "Plotinus argues for recurrence in *Enneads* 5.7.1–3, by saying that there is only a finite number of seminal reasons (*logoi*). So when as many creatures have been produced as there are seminal reasons, a new period and a new *kosmos* will have to start, containing the same creatures" (Sorabji, *Time, Creation, and the Continuum,* 186). Once again, we are back to the Pythagorean great year, which Plotinus called the *periodos pantos,* which Stephen MacKenna calls the "entire soul-period," and which A. H. Armstrong renders as the "whole revolution of the universe" (*Enneads,* trans. MacKenna, 407; trans. Armstrong, 5:225). Although Nietzsche never mentioned Plotinus as a predecessor in this regard, his idea, which we will look at in chapter 7, of eternal return as a finite set of cycles that must be re-created as a set over and over again, reduplicates the most specific feature of Plotinus's version of the doctrine. What I find most fascinating about Plotinus is that his articulation of the three emanations or hypostases (i.e., the One, the Intellectual Principles, and the World-Soul), so perfectly reproduces and heightens the tension in Plato's thought between the purity of Parmenidean stasis and the endless contamination of Heraclitean becoming. The need to find a general architectonic metaphor for the interlocking relations between the three hypostases is what led him, I surmise, to the striking image of the *Khôragus*. Perhaps more successfully than Plato, Plotinus differentiated the eternity of the One, which Plotinus etymologically unpacks as the *Aion* as *aéi-on* or "ever-being," and the eternal becoming of the World-Soul, whose rotating motion through the "soul-period" provides an eternally recurrent image in time of the timeless stasis of the One outside of time (cf. Festugière, 267). Plotinus fully explored the crucial time-fetishes of the *Timaeus*. It is as though the *Enneads* depict the last departing image of the ancient doctrine as it drifted into the remote past. Between the inorganic life of the eternal One and the eternal duration of living matter Plotinus tried somehow to integrate the aporia and the fetish of time and to think their difference.

Plotinus's account of the birth of time from eternity is curious above all because it ends up discovering that time seems to have a kind of infinite latency or gestation period within eternity, and that any talk of a "first stirring" of time in eternity leads to the aporia:

How Time emerged we can scarcely call upon the Muses to relate since they were not in existence then — perhaps not even if they had been....

Time at first — in reality before that "first" was produced by desire of succession — Time lay, though not yet as Time, in the Authentic Existent together with the Cosmos itself; the Cosmos also was merged in the Authentic and motionless within it. But there was an active participle there, one set on governing itself and realizing itself (= the All-Soul), and it chose to aim at something more than its present: it stirred from its rest, and the Cosmos stirred with it. (*Enneads* 3.7.11, trans. MacKenna)

Perhaps in an effort to refine the image that might reflect the paradox of this initial motionless stirring, to make more vivid and graspable the One's enigmatic desire for something beyond its own present, Plotinus continues the above argument by describing the "first stirring" of the "active principle" that will become the World Soul of the Cosmos as being most like a master who decides to disguise himself as a servant, who undresses himself in order to dress himself with a lesser raiment. Since this is all by way of prelude to my presentation of the *Khôragus*, which comes earlier in the *Enneads*, we might reasonably interpret the following passage as an actor dressing for his role, just about to come on stage: "To bring this Cosmos into being, the Soul first laid aside its eternity and clothed itself with Time; this world of its fashioning it then gave over to be a servant to Time, making it at every point a thing of Time, setting all its progressions within the bournes of Time" (trans. MacKenna). In Plotinus's text, not only is time, famously, the moving image of eternity (*tou aionos tòn chrónon eînai*), but perhaps more interestingly eternity is conversely, and inseparably, the only barely moving, almost totally static, image of time. And because all of this must be projected against the temporal horizon of eternal return, this enigmatic, unsayable difference is precisely what must have happened an infinite number of times already. The entire cycle may really be like a theatrical production of inconceivable grandeur, and above all one that knows itself as an ironic time-fetish that says the unsayable aporetic difference between time and eternity.

The most peculiar feature of Plotinus's cosmology is the curious fact that in his unpacking of Plato, the *khôra* or container of the World-Soul would always have to be in two places at once: at once outside and inside the One, always already there on the outside and yet also already about to spring from within the One. Like Heidegger's Anaximander, whose fragments do *and* do not say the aporetic time-question of ontological difference ("The Anaximander Fragment," 42), the Plotinus I read does *and* does not say that *khôra* is a time-fetish. The enigmatic temporality of the matter contained in the *khôra* seems clearly to come into view in the following passage:

Now if Matter is such a receptacle and nurse, all generation is distinct from it; and since all the changeable lies in the realm of generation, Matter, existing before all generation, must exist before all change.

"Receptacle" and "nurse"; then it receives its identity; it is not subject to modification. Similarly, if it is (as again we read) "the ground on which individual things appear and disappear," and so, too, if it is "a place" [*khôra*], a "base." The description may be challenged as situating the Ideas in space [*topos*]; yet to Matter it attributes no condition but merely probes after its distinctive manner of being. (*Enneads* 3.6.13, trans. MacKenna)

It is important to recall that in the third *Ennead* Plotinus is very keen on the metaphor of the mirror as a way of explaining the relation of the mode of existence of matter, whose reality in relation to the Intellectual Principles thus becomes most like the relation of the reflected image to the paradigm. The problem, of course, is that these specular metaphors betray the specular simultaneity of "before" and "after," which means that the model and the image come to presence together, joined in the same disjointed present. When it comes to the temporality of matter, it would appear that the specular copy precedes the model. What seems to emerge here is the possibility that something, some active principle or energy, may be moving back and forth, in and out, of a material realm that preexists (or coexists with) the principle itself. In any case, the *khôra* as the material trace of time seems at every temporal point to be on both sides of the mirror. Of course there must be no attribution of matter's temporality, which must somehow "exist before all change," and there must always be more probing into the *khôra* as the name of the unsayable difference between time and eternity.

We should note here as well that, although Plotinus's tractates were first presented to the world by his disciple Porphyry thirty years after the master's death, the frequency, persistence, and the highly idiomatic character of the text's concern with the nonconceptual, nonempirical thing that is *khôra* would appear to guarantee that this is certainly Plotinus's own usage and not some derivative or secondary feature of his thought. But regardless of who authored this detailed

unfolding of the dimensions or *diastema* (3.6.18) of the *khôra,* it goes
to the heart of the way Plato is read in the *Enneads.* The *khôra* guided
Plotinus (or whoever wrote the text) to an overall visual image of the
cosmos, a daring world-picture that is put into motion through infinite world-cycles. Not only does Plotinus dare to situate the topology
of the *khôra* "in the middle between matter [*hyle*] and form itself
[*eidos*]" (3.6.17, trans. Armstrong), or, in MacKenna's clearer phrasing, "midway between bare underlie and Pure Idea," not only does he
understand the paradoxicality of the time-fetish; what is significant
is that he dares to go still further and visualize the appearance of the
total system.

There are some other elements from Plato that are just as important
to Plotinus in coming to the image of the *Khôragus.* First, however, let
us turn to the image itself. Plotinus is speaking in *Ennead* 1.6.7 of the
thinker's imaginative vision of the One, the first hypostasis, the contemplation of which becomes possible only after the rigors of *sophro-
syne* and *katharsis.* Plotinus emphasizes the "invisible" character of
this vision of the One, which constitutes nothing less than "Absolute
beauty in Its essential integrity." Let us consider two translations of
the same text:

1.

Beholding this Being — the *Choragus* of all Existence, the Self-Intent that
gives forth and never takes — resting, rapt, in the vision and possession of
so lofty a loveliness, growing to Its likeness, what Beauty can the Soul yet
lack? [It is MacKenna, the translator, who preserves the Greek word.]

2.

If then one sees That which provides for all and remains itself, if he abides
in the contemplation of this kind of beauty and rejoices in being made
like it, how can he need any other beauty? [Armstrong]

While MacKenna regards *Khôragus* as untranslatable, Armstrong simply elides it; which is really quite extraordinary in itself, especially
since Armstrong has apparently devoted decades to his translation of
Plotinus. Perhaps this indicates a certain Parmenidean turn of phrase
on Armstrong's part, which predisposes the translation to a certain

inorganic abstractness in lieu of a word that connotes "abundance," a "full and extensive production." In any case, for a human subject to think about the eternal itself is effectively to behold in thought the *tò Kalòn,* the highest Beauty. Above all, however, the vision of the *Khôragus* is a vision of time and the world of becoming as the gift of the One, of "That which gives forth [*dídosi*] and never takes." But what can this gift be in its originary state but the coming to presence of time and matter? The immensity of this gift is what makes Its Beauty absolute. It would appear that the World Soul returns eternally only by virtue of the fact that, in each cycle, the One gives Its gift absolutely, without hope of return. Every time the cycle of becoming reaches its endpoint, there is another gift, or more precisely, the return of the same gift. And each time it is only because the gift is pure and absolute that there can be the eternal contamination that is the coming to presence of a cosmos. This pure gift takes the form of a circle, but it does so only inadvertently; only by giving a gift outside the circle of exchange is the circle achieved.

What is most beautiful about the One is Its gift, which takes us back to that first stirring of time; which in turn means that the gift of the *Khôragus* somehow includes the *khôra,* which is always already given; and Plotinus uses exactly the same language to speak of the subsisting nature of both *khôra* and *Khôragus.* We might say that the gift emanates, and that the *khôra* is inseparable from the first emergence of the active principle as it emerges from the One.

Khôragus (or *Choregus*) means the one who leads the chorus, the one who, according to Liddell and Scott, occupies an Athenian office responsible for "the defraying of the cost of solemn public choruses," which is doubtless related to its other meaning: "means for providing choroi," and so, generally, "abundance of money and other external means, fortune." Although they do not cite Plotinus's usage, Liddell and Scott do give two instances from Aristotle: one in the *Politics* (7.14) that means "abundance," or "abundant supply," and a second in the *Poetics* (14.3) that means generally "apparatus, for the stage." It should already be apparent that *Khôragus,* in the very specific usage of Plotinus, names a tremendous reserve or reservoir from whence springs the gift, and that the gift of the rich theatrical entrepreneur lies at the heart of Plotinus's vision of the emergent event of Being that Heidegger calls *Ereignis*. The *Khôragus* is the time-fetish within the time-fetish of the *khôra*, which is to say the fetishlike affirmation of a word and an image for the aporia of time.

We should also note that the Athenian office of the *Khôragus*, who was responsible for the theatrical life of the community, was largely replaced in Athenian culture after 325 B.C. "They seem to reappear in the Roman period," writes Sir Arthur Pickard-Cambridge, and are alluded to as late as 97 A.D. by Plutarch (*The Dramatic Festivals of Athens*, 74). It is difficult to speculate whether or not Plotinus's choice of just this word, in just this context, during the first half of the third century, was really as idiosyncratic as it would appear. Is there some biographical or historical connection long since lost that might have explained its apparent oddity? In lieu of a better explanation, I will simply offer two Platonic sources that may once again underlie Plotinian writing.

First and foremost is the famous passage in the *Phaedrus* on the highest beauty as *ekphanestaton kai erasmiôtaton*, "most radiant and most enchanting" (250 d), which is to say that which alone constitutes the unveiling of Being or the One. Heidegger's paraphrase of this passage is helpful: "It is rather what is most luminous and what thereby most draws us on and liberates us" (*Nietzsche I*, trans. Krell, 197). What radiates in the realm of appearance betokens a radiance infinitely brighter in the realm of thought, which is "the direction," as Heidegger implies, of *ekphanestaton*, a "standing out from" and "moving beyond" appearance (*phainestai*).

The second Platonic passage involves precisely that turn toward the *eidos* and the light of the Ideas in the famous allegory of the cave in *The Republic*. At the very moment when Socrates announces the soul's turn away from the delusions of representation and toward "the contemplation of essence and the brightest region of being" (518 d), he compares the rotarylike motion of the soul to "the scene-shifting *periakteon* in the theatre." I have discussed this image elsewhere (*Daemonic Figures*, 67–79), and want here only to suggest that Plotinus's theatrical turn of phrase may well have been a conscious allusion to this primal scene of Platonic reflection. Given the precision of Plotinus's other allusions, not only the *khôra* but the periact may lie behind the *Khôragus*. The periact was a mechanical device in the ancient Greek theater that consisted of a large triangular prism that was rotated from one of its three sides to the other in order to indicate topographical scene changes to the audience. The *Khôragus* seems strangely at home amid the nuts and bolts of the theater.

In Plotinus the world-child *Aion* becomes the *Khôragus,* the stage-master, where the entire universe is his stage. Moreover, in the process of articulating this complex allegory, the *Enneads* bring to the forefront all the latent contradictions and aporias that we saw in the basic Parmenidean-Heraclitean opposition. Plotinus continues Plato's loosening of the bonds that hold Being from within itself and that would presumably forestall any stirrings of coming-to-presence. In his effort to differentiate what *is* eternal from what *lives* eternally, Plotinus demonstrates precisely the opposite, which is that the determination of ontological difference is itself delusory insofar as it always presupposes having overcome the aporia of time. Since there is no true time, no pure, nonderivative, uncontaminated time to which we could contrast the calculable time of our duration, the very idea of distinguishing Being from beings remains a presumption for the future to decide, if it is to be decided at all. Curiously poised between the unpredictable springing forth of becoming in Heraclitus and the majestic hypostasis of Being in Parmenides, Plotinus may prove, at the end of the day, the most complete and rigorous theorist of the time-fetish and its aporia, in other words, the most complete thinker of eternal recurrence in Western culture.

Since I want to begin to turn toward Ovid and the cults of Bacchus in late paganism, it is interesting to note the presence of Dionysus in the text of Plotinus. I alluded earlier to Plotinus's characteristic habit of speaking, à la the allegory of Plato's cave, of the world of becoming as a delusory realm that could best be compared to images in a mirror. Although this is consistent with Plato's thinking, it remains a specifically Plotinian usage. Perhaps the clue to understanding the larger dynamic of this image, which we might also link to the actor (or active principle) before his dressing-room mirror, is to be found in Plotinus's discussion of the soul's descent into the world of becoming, which he compares to "the mirror of Dionysus": "But the souls of men see their images as if in the mirror of Dionysus and come to be on that level with a leap from above: but even these are not cut off from their own principle and from intellect" (*Ennead* 4.3.12, trans. Armstrong). As Armstrong points out in his gloss on this passage, the later Neoplatonists had developed a complex cosmological allegory from the story of how the Titans lured the child Dionysus with a mirror, tore him to pieces, and ate him. But of course Zeus avenged his son, and Dionysus was reborn. The child's seduction by its own mirror image is Plotinus's figure for the soul's separation from itself at the moment of its descent into becoming; for as Plotinus goes on to say, not only does part of the soul remain in heaven, the apparent "cut" is part of a larger suture, which he calls "one harmony with its circuit," where the "circuit" (*periphoràn*) is that of the entire "soul-period." Plotinus's "circuit" of eternal recurrence is thus a tremendous theatrical event, the hyper-Wagnerian "total work of art," in which the *Khôragus* disseminates the *logoi* through the World Soul, whose scattering is precisely the Dionysian "leap" into time and becoming. What the *Khôragus* must inevitably stage and restage is the production of the Dionysian "leap downward" (trans. MacKenna), which is the cycle of the total system.

It is tempting to speculate that this Dionysian characterization of the total system may register the deep undercurrents during the third century linking Neoplatonic cosmology and the Dionysian mystery cults. We will look closely at what that context might have been later in the next chapter. Let us conclude this brief discussion of Greek thought with what may be one of the very last images in the West of the Neoplatonic cosmology. It is Yggdrasill, "The Mundane Tree," the World-Tree, the world in the image of the ash tree, which the ancients believed lived longer than any other, and under the branches of which the gods meet in the Old Norse *Prose, or Younger Edda,* "which is generally ascribed to the celebrated Snorri Sturalson, who was born of a distinguished Icelandic family, in the year 1178, and after leading a turbulent and ambitious life, and being twice the supreme magistrate of the Republic, was killed A.D. 1241" (Mallet, *Northern Antiquities,* 377). Although the *Prose Edda* was not published until 1665, its accounts of Norse mythology in fifty-three chapters provide an extraordinary glimpse into the afterlife of pagan culture in the early medieval period. The drawing of Yggdrasill reproduced here (figure 1) is from an 1847 reprint of Bishop Percy's translation (1770) of Paul Henri Mallet's *Monuments de la mythologie et de la poésie des Celtes, et particulièrement des anciens Scandinaves* (1756). Yggdrasill has a rich history as a cosmological symbol. In his extensive annotations to this 1847 Bohn Library Reprint, I. A. Blackwell says that one of the early commentators on the *Edda*, Finn Magnusen, derived Yggdrasill "from *y*, cognate with *úr*, moisture, rain; when *yg*, *ygg*, was afterwards formed, and *drasill*, from the verb *draga*, to carry (probably cognate with the German *tragen*, and the English *to drag*); or from *Ygg*, one of Odin's names and *drasill*, bearing; hence, according to Finn Magnusen, it would signify bearing (producing) rain, or bearing Odin" (*Northern Antiquities*, 570).

But before considering more closely the philology of this Norse time-fetish, let us turn to the end of the *Prose Edda*, to strophe 51, which describes the ekpyrotic death of the world year as the conflagration of the world-tree: "the fire reek raging around *Time's Nurse*" (my emphasis). I can only speculate that this astonishing metaphor of Yggdrasill as "Time's Nurse" is Sturalson's integration into Norse mythology of Plato's *khôra*, "the Mother and Receptacle of this generated world." It is the Norns, or Furies, who decree that Yggdrasill shall break asunder and burn in Ragnarök, the Twilight of the Gods. And they decree as well, in strophe 53, the renovation of the world: "There will arise out of the sea another earth most lovely and verdant with pleasant fields where the grain shall grow unsown."

This drawing does not depict the three Norns, the Parcae or Fates, whom we might imagine lingering near the *Torweg* or gateway arch that appears to channel the primordial alchemical elements and energies that circulate around the roots of the world-tree. The key to Yggdrasill lies in the Norns and in their names: *Urd, Verdandi,* and *Skuld*, which mean, respectively, past, present, and future. The root word for *Urd* and *Verdandi* is the verb *verda; ordïnn* is the past participle, and *verdandi* is the present participle. The Norse *verda* means "to become" and is related to the German *werden* and the Anglo-Saxon *weordan*. The Anglo-Saxon *Wyrdas*, which translates Norns,

1. *Yggdrasill, the Mundane Tree,* frontispiece to Paul Henri Mallet's
Northern Antiquities, trans. Bishop Percy, ed. I. A. Blackwell
(London: Henry A. Bohn, 1847).

or Destinies, thus makes the notion of becoming (*werden*) the core meaning of the English *weird,* as in Shakespeare's "Weird Sisters," the sisters of the eternal ring of becoming. *Skuld* derives from *skula* and is related to the English *shall.* And so, writes Blackwell, elaborating on Mallet's scholarship: "The three Norns regulate the destinies of gods and men; even Odin himself, who in the Ymerian myth is represented as the father of all, must submit to their decrees; which means to say, in other words, that there is an inevitable succession of events in time; Uncreated Time, Time without beginning or end — the Zeruane Akherene of the Persians — personified in its three moments of the Past, the Present, and the Future, as three maidens by the fountain of perennial life, being the only deity recognised" (*Northern Antiquities,* 494). It may well be that these Norse myths and images from around the turn of the first millennium are really translations of Plato and Neoplatonic elements into Old Norse, and may thus constitute, to use a metaphor of Walter Benjamin's, the last snapshot of a European paganism unfettered by Christianity and thus able to affirm eternal recurrence as the very stuff of language itself.

2

From Ovid to Titian:

Eternal Return and the Cult of

Bacchus and Ariadne

The most holy games to be celebrated with the greatest care and ceremony
are those in honor of Ceres, Liber, and Libera. CICERO, *In Verrem*

Even if, after death time [*aetas*] should collect
our materiality [*materiam*] and make it as it is now,
Even if the light of life [*lumina vitae*] were ours again,
even that would not concern us,
Once the thread of memory had been interrupted [*interrupta*].
LUCRETIUS

In the union of the two archetypal images, the divine pair of Dionysos and
Ariadne represent the eternal passage of *zoë* into and through the genesis of
living creatures. This occurs over and over again and is always, uninterrupt-
edly, present. C. KERÉNYI, *Dionysos*

In the history of religion the theology of eternal recurrence in the
West remains paradoxically unwritten, while at the same time we
might also conclude that it has been endlessly rewritten throughout
the Judeo-Christian tradition, which is nothing but the theology of
eternal return, shorn, as it were, à la Parmenides, from the world of
becoming. The good news of the Christians is that we come back to
ourselves, although there is confusion as to how and in what material

form. As Caroline Walker Bynum has shown, the central question in the Christian theology of resurrection concerned precisely the measure of proximity of the resurrected body to the body as it was in the world of becoming; in other words, upon which stage in the lifespan of one's bodily existence is the paradigm for one's resurrected body to be copied or revived (*The Resurrected Body in Western Christianity*)? "There's the rub," as Hamlet might interject, whether we are to find ourselves reborn, as it were, with orthodontic braces, or with a prosthetic pin in our hip? Recall that the resurrected Christ is a very material being with appetite, sensation, and reflection, no longer simply a human being but one with all the attributes of human perception he possessed at the moment of his death. It is tempting to regard this aspect of Christ's resurrection as his most Dionysian moment: the irreducibly embodied and material existence of the god in the realm of becoming through infinite cycles of finite worlds. The atemporal spiritual eternity of the Christian god ultimately betrayed, however, an impatience with the aporia of time and an unwillingness to pursue as far as Plotinus had the temporal horizon of the meaning of Being. From the vantage point of eternal return, the Christian god proclaims an old story: that god is the Son of Man, that god dies, and that man and god are reborn together. Augustine's rejection of eternal return in book 12 of *The City of God* may, however, have closed the door for centuries to the possibility of rethinking the essential identity of Dionysos and Christ.

The effort to understand the cultural and psychological reasons for vacillation on the part of thinkers and the intellectual public vis-à-vis the doctrine of return is always speculative, as in the case of Theunissen's remarks about Parmenides and the need to liberate his contemporaries from the burden of eternal recurrence. Surveying the fate of the doctrine in the ancient world, Richard Sorabji concludes: "The theory was not a source of consolation, but often an additional source of horror" (*Time, Creation, and the Continuum*, 190). Nietzsche's remark in his notebook during 1881 about the doctrine as "a selective principle, in the service of force (and barbarism!)" (*KSA* 10:646) should be understood as a historical fact, which is to say that we might begin to differentiate epochs according to their intellectual

daring with respect to the meaning of time, or their timidity in relation to their sense of the vitality of life. Although in general eternal
recurrence is certainly capable of making cowards of us all, there are
epochs where a certain intellectual realism and ironic cultural melancholy seem to coalesce in such a way as to provide a hospitable milieu
for the thought of the aporia of time.

The story I want to tell now concerns the revival in philosophy and
poetry of Pythagorean-Heraclitean-Stoic-Lucretian notions of ekpyrotic *Diakosmesis* (the preferred Stoic term for the great year), which
extended from the time of Cicero all the way into second- and third-
century Rome and beyond. Ovid's writing in the early first century
opened the most intense period of interest in the doctrine. This revival
was accompanied by a renaissance of the ancient Dionysian Greek
mystery cults, thanks in part to their reinvention by Ovid in terms of
the ancient Latin gods of the vine and of nature's mysteries, Liber Pater
and Libera, with whom he successfully merged Dionysus and Ariadne.
Although this remained an esoteric and intellectual cult, the Bacchic
mysteries of eternal recurrence left important traces in architecture
and in sarcophagal art, which we will consider in a moment. Students
of the period appear to agree that the trendsetter here was Cicero's
friend Nigidius Figulus, who was generally regarded as *Pythagoricus et
magus,* a Zoroastrian-style magus who taught the mysteries of Osiris-
Dionysius (cf. Carcopino, *La Basilique pythagoricienne,* 196–202; Rawson, *Intellectual Life in the Late Roman Republic,* 309–12; Kingsley,
Ancient Philosophy, Mystery and Magic, 324–25). At least three important elements contributed to Ovid's synthesis of a Heraclitean cosmology and the figure of Bacchus / Liber Pater: (1) Nigidius's revival
of Pythagorean cosmology and the Dionysian mysteries; (2) Lucretius's synthesis of Stoic cosmologies (on which, see Furley, *Cosmic
Problems;* and Myers, *Ovid's Causes*); and perhaps crucially, (3) the
growing popularity of the plebian cult of Liber, Libera, and Ceres
(on which, see Frazer, *Fasti of Ovid,* 3:105–10, and Bruhl, *Liber Pater*).
What emerged by the middle of the first century was a new cult of Bacchus / Liber Pater whose rituals and iconography were linked to the
esoteric doctrine of return. As Bruhl remarks, this cult was linked as

well to the republican idea, and thus to Dionysus as a figure of democracy: "Along with Ceres, the lawmaker, Liber was considered among the plebians as the god of liberty. They made offerings to him so that the liberty of the citizenry might be preserved. The very name of Liber predisposed itself to this function. . . . Dionysus was also in Greece a democratic god" (*Liber Pater*, 41–42). And for poets the name Liber had the additional advantage of being associated not only with the republican ideal but with the very composition of a "little book" or *liber*.

Although a certain democratic spirit of liberation may have inspired the vogue of eternal recurrence, the cult and its ideas survived the fall of the republic and lingered on, more or less esoterically, through the heyday of the empire and into its decline. "In reality," writes Frazer, "Liber and Libera were an ancient pair of native Italian deities, who, if we can trust the testimony of Augustine [*City of God*, bk. 4.11], presided over human seed, the god Liber presiding over the seed of men, and the goddess Libera presiding over the seed of women. The pair were worshiped together at the festival of the Liberalia on the seventeenth of March; and their heads are exhibited on the obverse and reverse respectively of coins (*denarii*) issued by L. Cassius about 79 B.C. In their portraits on the coins the god and goddess are clearly identified with Dionysus and his female partner [Ariadne]" (*Fasti of Ovid*, 3:109–10). Ovid flourished almost a century later, and the synthesis between Dionysus and Liber Pater remained one of the central subjects of his poetry.

There has always been something inherently dizzying about Pythagorean notions of a finite cosmos expanding and contracting through infinite time, perhaps even something revolutionary or disruptive. Aristotle remarked in *On the Heavens* (2.13) that the Pythagoreans had the temerity to think that the earth might *not* be at the center of the universe. And the Stoic cosmologists of Lucretius's time proposed the existence of an immense source of heat and light at the center of the cosmos. A sort of counterintuitive critical negation would appear to be the stock and trade of Pythagorean cosmologies and Dionysian mysteries. In other words, the secret history of eternal recurrence is always a kind of Dionysian "leap" into time's uncanny enigma. And although eternal recurrence as a religious doctrine is just another crude fetish, there is always the possibility that it could become an ironic poetic construction.

I want to begin looking at Ovid through the optic of an utterly preposterous question, one that knows that it is unanswerable from the outset: what might be the connection between the doctrine of return and Ovid's famous banishment from Rome in 8 A.D.? It is impossible to determine whether his crime or his offense to the Emperor Augustus was political, or sexual, or whether Augustus was pursuing a very focused and determined imperial censorship of the arts. During his exile on the shores of the Black Sea (where he continued to write until his death in 17 A.D.), Ovid studiously avoided revealing the actual nature of his crime. Book 2 of the *Tristia* or *Sorrows* is Ovid's defense of his poetical-moral practice, with its obvious sexual license. It is really the freedom of poetic expression, however, that is most at stake and not, apparently, or so Ovid repeatedly claims, something in his social conduct or lifestyle. The culmination of the *Tristia* may well be its poem "To Bacchus" in book 5, where Ovid laments his inability to attend the *celebrare poetae,* the convocation of the poets on March 17, the Liberalia, when they gather in order to sing the praises of Bacchus/Liber, the god whose double birth means that the Parcae have spun for him a double law. The poet calls upon Liber to reverse the imperial ban ("sway Caesar's power divine by thine own") and to bring him aid: *Fer, bone Liber, opem* (*Tristia* 5.3.37). In this case the abundance or fecundity of the vegetative god seems to offer Ovid the promise that "a second vine" may be suspended so that he might attend the train of Bacchants once again. Is this not a quiet, ironic hope of eternal return? (Recall that the first line of the *Tristia* contrasts the exile of the poet himself to the ability of his "little book" [*liber*] to make its way freely in the city.) Ovid hopes that Liber will notice he is missing and bring him back once more into his party: "come and lighten my misfortunes, fairest of gods, remembering that I am one of thine own [*unum de numero me memor esse tuo*]" (44).

Whether the license of his amorous poems fell afoul of the emperor's sensibility, or whether Ovid made an indiscreet allusion regarding a member of the imperial family, he had transgressed some sort of limit.

But could we not also understand this step over the line as a "leap" into a new experience of the meaning of time? At the risk of being overly attentive to Plotinus's notion of the Dionysian "leap" of the soul into coming-to-presence, we might look back to Ovid's earlier *Ars amatoria* where he dramatizes the lover's art of seduction through the figure of Bacchus *leaping* to console Ariadne, who has been abandoned by her lover Theseus on Naxos and has fallen into a dreamy despair. "I am here for you," cries Bacchus, and "down he leaped [*desilit*] from his chariot, lest the girl take fright at the tigers" (1:560). Ovid also refers to this scene at some length in the *Fasti* and mentions it in passing in "To Bacchus." This is of course the moment and the leap immortalized by Titian's *Bacchus and Ariadne* (1523; National Gallery, London), which we will consider more closely in a moment. As he leaps down in an amorous engagement in the world of becoming, the Bacchus of the *Ars amatoria* promises Ariadne that he will prove a "more faithful lover" (*cura fidelior*) than Theseus. Whatever stood for Ovid as being nearest to the core of his vocation as a poet transpired under the sign of Liber Pater: "*Ecce, suum vatem Liber vocat*" [Lo, Liber summons his bard] (1:525). Of Bacchus Ovid writes in the *Metamorphoses*: "No god is closer than he" [*nec enim praesentior illo / est deus*]. But how close, how proximate, how truly interior or in-dwelling is this god?

Perhaps Pythagoras's great speech in book 15 of the *Metamorphoses* may give us an insight into Ovid's ontology of the temporal dimensions of the self. The Heraclitean image of time as a river (*flumen*) appears at the outset to exclude any element of repetition, since it bears everything endlessly forward. Although on one level the cosmos appears like an ever-changing river, there is within the stream a dimension of soul-stuff that remains rigorously resistant to the relentless disseminative force of time. In short, we see that the river of time flows eerily in a circle:

There is nothing in all the world [*nihil est toto*] that keeps its form. All things are in a state of flux, and everything is brought into being [*labuntur tempora motu*] with a changing nature. Time itself flows on in constant motion, just like a river. For neither the river nor the swift hour can stop its course; but, as wave is pushed on by wave, and as each wave is both impelled by that behind and itself impels the wave in front, so time both flees and follows and is ever new. For that which once existed is no more, and that which was not has come to be; and so the whole round of motion is gone through again [*momentaque cuncta novantur*]. (15:178–85)

Ovid's word is *cunctus,* the whole cycle, the recurrence of the total system, within which nothing is *toto,* nothing is whole in the sense of having Being since everything incessantly changes form in becoming. It is the entirety of becoming that preserves its difference only within an overarching sameness. Pythagoras continues:

Nothing retains its own form; but Nature, the great renewer [*rerumque novatrix*], ever makes up forms from other forms. Be sure there's nothing perishes [*perit*] in the whole universe; it does but vary and renew its form. What we call birth is but a beginning to be other than what one was before; and death is but cessation of a former state. Though, perchance, things may shift from there to here and here to there, still do all things in their sum total remain unchanged [*summa tamen omnia constant*]. (252–58)

It is not only the finitude of the total system that remains constant, it is also the soul-stuff:

Our souls are deathless, and ever, when they have left their former seat, do they live in new abodes [*novis domibus*] and dwell in the bodies that have received them. (158–59)

Pythagoras then rehearses his prior incarnations, he himself having once been a certain Euphorbus who was slain by Menelaus in the Trojan War:

All things are changing; nothing dies. The spirit [*spiritus*] wanders, comes now here, now there, and occupies whatever form it pleases. From beasts it passes into human bodies, and from our bodies into beasts, but never perishes. And, as the pliant wax is stamped with new designs [*novis facilis signatur*], does not remain as it was before nor preserve the same form, but is still the selfsame wax, so do I teach that the soul [*animam*] is ever the same, though it passes into ever-changing bodies. (165–72)

The pliant waxlike stuff of the soul remains constant even as the imprint it receives, that is, the body it inhabits, is constantly changing. From cycle to cycle there are thus two levels of sameness: the finite limits of the general system, and the quantity of soul-stuff within it. That is why Pythagoras rails against animal sacrifice and meat eating and thus also against "the avenging altars of Bacchus" (114–15), where animal sacrifice is prominent. Ovid's Bacchus is rather vengeful in the *Metamorphoses,* and his most significant appearance there involves his reprisals against Pentheus, who is slain by his mother and other bacchants for his infidelity to the god (3:510–732). Whatever Ovid may have thought of vegetarianism, his fidelity to Bacchus as his tutelary spirit would appear unaffected by these dietary considerations. The more crucial point, I believe, is that the in-dwelling proximity of Bacchus ("no one is nearer than he") seems most closely linked to Ovid's sense of an inner selfsameness of some part of the self, whether it is *spiritus* or *anima,* a part that cannot be brought to consciousness and that eludes self-reflection, something that has presence but that cannot be made present. It is this temporal modality of the poet's Dionysian inner existence and participation in a realm of recurrent sameness that lies at the heart of Ovid's sense of the Pythagorean doctrine.

We will return to these moments in Ovid again in chapter 3, for they stand at the center of Shakespeare's poetic thinking about eternal recurrence.

Let us now begin to turn to the Bacchic cults themselves, and particularly to the preeminence there of the story of Bacchus and Ariadne. In the *Fasti* Ovid writes of Bacchus's encounter with Ariadne on Naxos, where he hears her plaint, then promises her his love, renames her the goddess Libera and bestows upon her a golden ring of nine jewels, which at her death he placed in the heavens as a ring of stars, the Corona Borealis or Cnossian Crown (3:459–516). Later in book 3 Ovid depicts the Liberalia and makes a number of interesting reflections, such as the reason old women follow the cult is "that age is more addicted to wine, and loves the bounty of the teeming vine" (766), or that the reason why boys wear "the gown of liberty" on March 17 is "because thou art Liber, the gown of liberty is assumed and a freer [*liberior*] life is entered upon under thine auspices" (778). And he concludes by asking Liber to "fill the sails of my poetic art [*ingenio*]" (790). And what fills Ovid's poetic art, what lies at the heart of his idea of "a freer life," is his secret poetic history of eternal recurrence.

It is thanks to two landmark books, whose significance to the history of eternal recurrence cannot be exaggerated—Jerôme Carcopino's *La Basilique pythagoricienne de la porte majeure* and Adrien Bruhl's *Liber Pater: Origine et expansion du culte dionysiaque à Rome et dans le monde romain*—that we might begin to see more clearly the extent to which the revival of Neopythagorean cosmologies, Ovid's poetry, and the figure of Bacchus all contributed to a widespread, though nevertheless esoteric, fascination with the Liber/Libera story that was expressed in numerous instances of sarcophagal and funerary art, as well as in the construction by the Emperor Claudius in 53 A.D. of a Pythagorean basilica at the main gate to Rome on the road to Naples. Carcopino demonstrates, for example, how influential the *Metamorphoses* were to the design of the temple, and how important a role was played there by motifs of the Dionysian mysteries with its bacchants and triumphal processions (e.g., 155-59). Bruhl, on the other hand, reveals the extraordinary appeal that Bacchus and Ariadne had as a sarcophagal motif, whose esoteric teaching we are now able to understand more clearly. As Bruhl reminds us, we must be wary of associating the actual practice of Dionysian mysteries (e.g., the unveiling of the phallus) and their literary expression in Ovid and other poets with their visual expression as a decorative motif (144). All of the scenes we have thus discussed relating to the various myths involving Bacchus and Ariadne, as well as to the initiation rites and their accompanying paraphernalia, were repeatedly used in the funerary and sacred art of the period. Since Bruhl's study was published in 1953, there have been two subsequent surveys of Dionysian sarcophagal art (by Robert Turcan in one volume and the authoritative work by Friedrich Matz in four). What has become unmistakably clear is that late Roman paganism regarded various episodes in the life of Dionysus, and above all his rescue of Ariadne, as providing the imagery and narrative form that gave meaning to the experience of death, burial, and the afterlife as well. Whether they were initiates of the cult or not, or whether much of this sculpture was merely a style-conscious statement, those families who commissioned such work and those whose lives were literally permeated by these images (and one need only consult Matz's four volumes of plates to confirm just how widespread the fashion was), it is difficult to imagine that there were not a great many people who clearly saw a melancholy allegory of resurrection as Ariadne arose from a sorrowful sleep beneath the loving gaze of the god.

The cult of Liber Pater, which flourished as late as the sixth century in what are today France and Germany, has nevertheless left surprisingly few traces upon our cultural history. It remains an essentially undiscovered legacy, and thus it points toward another beginning, an ideology of resurrection and the life everlasting *within* the world of becoming, awakening once again in the material stuff of this world rather than in the so-called "law of the Spirit of life" [*nomos ton pneumatos tes zoes*] of which Saint Paul speaks (Romans 8.1). Instead of being "set free from the law of sin and death" [*hamartia kai thanaton*] by Jesus Christ, the mystery cult and its imagery wistfully suggest that Dionysus offers the promise of freedom within the world of becoming, not in the disembodied spiritual life of the eternal. One god promises to guide you through the endless cycles of life/death, while the other promises, à la Parmenides, a stasis beyond all becoming.

And that is why I believe this sarcophagal sculpture from the second century A.D. (figure 2) is so important as an allegory of another beginning, the trace of a Heraclitean worldview, an Ovidian world-image, that somehow remained too esoteric, too ironic, and thus perhaps too remote and impersonal to survive the ancient world. Matz dates it around 170 A.D. (3:378–81). Here the tiger rests near the foot of the god, with Silenus perched in a tree, while Ariadne quietly awakens, and everywhere drapes the heaviness of the vine. Of all the many representations I have seen of this scene, this version captures best what I regard as the essence of the sarcophagal time-fetish: a dream of rebirth and resurrection situated fully within the world of becoming. In its almost domestic rendering of the archetypal story, the reawakening of the dead takes on all the charm of an amorous tryst. It is interesting to note that Titian also depicted a reposing Ariadne in very much the posture of this sarcophagal relief, which is representative of

2. *Bacchus Coming to Ariadne.* Sarcophagus of the Villa Medici, Rome.
Reproduced from Adrien Bruhl, *Liber Pater* (Paris: E. de Boccard, 1953).

dozens like it over several centuries. Bataille reproduces the painting,
Bacchanalia, in his *Tears of Eros* (113). This posture of supine languor
is usually depicted in connection with Bacchus's arrival on the scene,
while Titian has appropriated them into two separate scenes.

   Albert Henrichs has spoken to this question of the intimacy of the
Dionysian cults: "Dionysus, *deus praesentissimus,* 'the god of the most
immediate presence,' reveals himself more, more ostentatiously, and
with greater emphasis on his anthropomorphic properties than any
other Greek god—witness the frequency of epiphany scenes in Dio-
nysiac myth and art, and the close ritual resemblance between the
god and his worshippers in cult" ("Human and Divine in Dionysus,"
19). Henrichs is speaking of the Greek cults, but what he says is even
more applicable to the Roman Bacchus. Another motif we have not
spoken of involves the infant Dionysus and the ministrations of his
loving attendants, which is an image closely related to the unveiling of
the phallic fetish. Such intersections between the Dionysian mysteries

and the emerging cult of Jesus Christ attest above all to a general fascination in late paganism with the nature of the afterlife. The history of eternal recurrence was effectively driven underground in the generations after Plotinus, who brought to a close the period of the revival of the doctrine that had begun with the plebian cult of Liber Pater c. 100 B.C. The succeeding centuries witnessed the ascendancy of the Christians and the destruction of the traces of the ancient cults.

I want to turn finally to two images, one that marks the termination of the epoch of the *deus praesentissimus* and another that signals his leap back onto the stage of European culture. First, there is the statue of the Syrian Dionysus (figure 3), an androgynous figure of Bacchus from the early fourth century which was discovered in an excavation in 1908 in the Syrian Sanctuary on the Janiculum, which is a prominent ridge on the west bank of the Tiber. The priests of the cult managed to hide only this solitary object, and unfortunately the Christians who destroyed the temple demolished everything else beyond recognition (Bruhl, 259). The Bacchants must not have had much time to prepare for the onslaught, only enough to hide this single statue, which somehow they knew was the one that had to be saved from destruction. Bruhl quotes one historian's speculation that this statue is "a representation of Aion, the alexandrine god of Eternity" (Bruhl, 259). This is obviously not an abstract and disembodied Aion but the figure of an infinitely erotic lassitude. With his empty cantharus and his thyrsus in his hands, we might imagine that our Syrian Dionysus is gazing at Ariadne, as he did on the sarcophagus, and that her statue and others must have been lost in the raid. This Dionysus is an androgynous object of desire, in whom all viewers see their other. Like the "master-mistress" of Shakespeare's Sonnets, this figure of Bacchus is the image not of eternity as an eternal present but of eternal recurrence, of the eternal and inexhaustible desire of eternity for the world of becoming.

Perhaps the best commentary on this statue comes from Friedrich Hölderlin, who unfortunately never saw it but whose poem "Bread and Wine" seems uncannily to have anticipated its most essential meaning. The poem is Hölderlin's attempt to reinvent another beginning, to find his way back to that fork in the road of history

3. Statue of Bacchus from the Syrian Sanctuary on the Janiculum.
Musée des Thermes, Rome. Reproduced by permission of Museo
Nazionale Romano.

that led thinking and poetry away from the thought of infinite
coming-to-presence, in order to invent, as he calls it in "The Oldest
System-Program of German Idealism," "a new mythology of reason,"
and more specifically a non-Christian and Dionysian mythology (cf.
Schulte-Sasse, *Theory in Practice*, 73). In stanza 9 Hölderlin describes

Dionysus as reconciling day and night and as leading "the stars of the sky eternally upward, and down again" and as bringing "the trace of the gods departed / Down to the godless below, into the midst of their gloom" (trans. Michael Hamburger [slightly modified]). But what links this poem to this remarkable statue is Hölderlin's account in the concluding stanza of the coming of the Syrian, about whose identity there need be no confusion, and no speculation either about a Christian-pagan synthesis; no, there can be no mistake, Hölderlin's Syrian is *this* Syrian Dionysus:

Comes the Syrian and down into our gloom bears his torch.
Blissful, the wise see it; in souls that were captive there gleams a
Smile, and their eyes shall yet thaw in response to the light.

This too is the dream of another beginning, the beginning of a new interpretation of the meaning of time and eternity.

The second image is Titian's well-known Ovidian painting *Bacchus and Ariadne* (frontispiece). Shakespeare probably did not know this painting, but Nietzsche probably did, even though he nowhere mentions it. He wanted, of course, to write a poetic drama, more precisely a "satyr-play," about the first meeting of Bacchus and Ariadne, their marriage and other bacchanals. At one point in his notebooks for summer 1883 he sketches a scene that recalls something like Titian's painting: "Dionysus on a tiger . . . the skull of a goat . . . a panther . . . Ariadne dreaming—'abandoned by the hero, I dream of the super-hero [*Über-Helden*].' Not to mention Dionysus" (*KSA* 10:433). Still at work on the project several years later, Nietzsche imagines Ariadne from the god's point of view: " 'Oh, Ariadne,' " says Dionysus, " 'you yourself are the Labyrinth: one never gets out of you' " (*KSA* 12:510). The meaning is clear: although she saved Theseus from the Minotaur's labyrinth, there is no exit from the labyrinth of becoming, even for a god. So let us reflect for a moment on a painting that must have been in Nietzsche's thoughts as he struggled with his abortive "satyr-play."

All the interest lies, of course, in Bacchus's extraordinary leap from his chariot, which, as we saw earlier, derives from the *Ars amatoria*. Titian suspends his right foot in midair, his head askew and lowered with the force of the downward leaping motion. John Keats was struck by "the swift bound of Bacchus," which he read as an allegory of his own experience of "the pleasant flow / Of words" that leap to mind on opening a picture-book (cf. *Sleep and Poetry*, lines 331–38). It was in his last book, *Problems in Titian*, that Erwin Panofsky analyzed the iconography of this leap and considered its relation to ancient Roman sarcophagal art (*Problems in Titian*, 141–44); and we will consider this in a moment. First, however, what is most striking about the leap is the way it focuses attention on Bacchus's tender gaze toward Ariadne; and the reason why the god's posture appears so irregular is that he is intent on keeping his eyes on her even as he is leaping from the chariot that is coming to a rest. The effect of the leap is to focus attention on the gaze of the lovers; the leap literally pulls us into the vector of force of the gaze. Look at the sarcophagal sculpture once again, where the gaze of the god and Ariadne's turning to answer it define the focal point of the work. The same is true of Titian's work as well, which unleashes all the force and expressivity of the gaze into the bounding leap of the god.

The leap of Titian's Bacchus activates and gives expression to something very elemental about the myth and the esoteric doctrine about time and rebirth to which it is so closely linked. I want to focus on the linkage between the leap, the gaze, and the active principle that cause Being to spring toward the world of becoming. When Panofsky considers the possibility of an iconographic link between the leaping Bacchus and the Roman sarcaphagi, the only connection he can find is a rather remote one to a vague resemblance to the posture of a figure of Orestes. Panofsky thanks a colleague for bringing that sarcophagus to his attention and implies that he never really reviewed the relevant material himself. In fact, he says only that some "show Bacchus quietly descending, not leaping, from his chariot" (141). So, on the one hand, Panofsky's remarks on the painting are interesting insofar as they focus on the leap, on the *desilit* in Ovid's text, as the key to the painting's central and most idiomatic statement, while on the other hand, Panofsky never considered the larger issues that are raised by the many sarcophagi relating to Bacchus and Ariadne, regardless of whether or not there's even a chariot. If he had, he might have come to recognize that the leap of Titian's Bacchus is really an esoteric allegory of eternity's longing for time and time's longing for eternity. No less than the Syrian statue, Titian presents Bacchus as Aion. Unlike the priests of Bacchus, Titian may never have known the esoteric doctrine of eternal return. Perhaps it was his sense of the energy and dynamism of Ovid's text, which, as Panofsky shows, Titian knew intimately, or perhaps it was his genius as a painter interested in the torsion and momentum of the human body. Whatever it was, Titian understood that something essential about the relation of Bacchus and Ariadne could be depicted only through the figure of the god leaping in midair to save the human from despair, from losing herself in the infinite distance that seems to stretch out beyond Theseus's ship, which seems literally to be scurrying away from her outstretched hand. The leap and the gaze pull her back from an imminent nothingness and into the cymbal-filled din of the bacchanal. In the sky above them the ring of stars appears enigmatically to suggest that all of this is about something esoteric: the ring of recurrence and the eternal cycles of becoming.

There is yet one final possible source for both the leaping Bacchus of Titian and Hölderlin's Syrian Dionysus who illuminates our earthly gloom with the gleaming torch of his presence. Is it not obvious that Bacchus's leap is part of the frenzied dance of the revelers? And is not Hölderlin's point that Dionysus is an allegory of the movement of the starry cosmos that brings the immensity of the natural world into some relation with human history? The leap is a kind of dance, and the dance is an allegory of the disruptive and unsettling relation of the time of universal nature to the time of human existence. These elements are already present in an incantation for the god's appearance that is spoken by the chorus in Sophocles' *Antigone;* and like Plotinus, Sophocles too addresses Dionysus as the *Khôragus* who guides the universal motion of the heavens:

Hail, leader [*Khôragus*] of the dance of fire-breathing stars,
Master of the voices heard by night,
Son of Zeus, appear,
King, with your attendant Thyiads [Maenads], who in their frenzy
Dance all night long in honor of their lord Iacchus [Bacchus].
(lines 1147–52, trans. slightly modified)

II

Shakespeare

I saw that the moods and passions mirrored [in the Sonnets] were absolutely essential to Shakespeare's perfection as an artist writing for the Elizabethan stage, and that it was in the curious theatre conditions of that stage that the poems themselves had their origin. I remember what joy I had in feeling that these wonderful Sonnets [. . .] were no longer isolated from the great aesthetic energies of Shakespeare's life, but were an essential part of his dramatic activity, and revealed something of the secret of his method.

OSCAR WILDE, "The Portrait of Mr. W.H."

Appearance is the actual and only reality of things. I do not posit "appearance" in opposition to "reality," but, on the contrary, take appearance as that reality which resists [*wiedersetzt*] transformation into an imaginative "world of truth."

NIETZSCHE, *Nachlass*

3

"Shakespearances"; or, The War with Time

Against the backdrop of the history of eternal recurrence, Francis Meres's remark about Shakespeare's Sonnets (some of which had presumably circulated in manuscript during the late 1590s), now appears particularly prescient in its keen sense of the Pythagorean drift of Shakespeare's thinking: "As the soul of Euphorbus was thought to live in Pythagoras, so the sweet witty soul of Ovid lives in mellifluous and honey-tongued Shakespeare. Witness his *Venus and Adonis;* his *Lucrece;* his sugared sonnets among his private friends, etc." (*Palladis Tamia: Wit's Treasury* [1598]). Meres was a thirty-two-year-old Anglican divine with M.A.'s from Oxford and Cambridge when he wrote this comparison of English authors to the ancients. The above remarks continue with praise for Shakespeare's excellence in comedy and tragedy: "For comedy, witness his *Gentlemen of Verona;* his *Errors;* his *Love's Labour's Lost;* his *Midsummer Night's Dream;* and his *Merchant of Venice.* For tragedy: his *Richard II., Richard III., Henry IV., King John, Titus Andronicus,* and his *Romeo and Juliet.* As Epius Stolo [actually, Aelius Stilo, c. 100 B.C.] said that the muses would speak with Plautus's tongue if they would speak Latin; so I say that the muses would speak with Shakespeare's fine filed phrase if they were to speak English." Like Ovid and Plautus in relation to Latin, Shakespeare is able to draw from the resources of the English language an Ovidian sweetness and music, and from Plautus a dramatic ability to give expression to carefully differentiated states of comic and tragic experience. These are no more than sketchy intuitions, but they seem to me uncannily to anticipate my theme concerning Shakespeare's place in the history of eternal return, and more generally his highly self-conscious role as the reanimator, as it were, of the ancient world. Meres pursues his gathering of the olive branches of Pallas Athena in ancient and modern times not only in literature but in painting and music as well, for his thesis is that English art and letters are worthy of the ancients for the simple reason that they reembody the ancients with such accuracy.

As far as I can tell, the only critic to make this argument before me, and to take Meres's remarks seriously, was Sidney Lee, who argued in "Ovid and Shakespeare's Sonnets" (1909) that "the last lines of the last book of Ovid's long poem gave Shakespeare a cue for his vaunt of eternal fame. A mass of earlier lines in the same book [15] presents a series of subtle conceptions about Time and Nature which Shakespeare's Sonnets absorb no less distinctly" ("Ovid and Shakespeare's Sonnets," 125). This is an extraordinarily powerful suggestion, and I shall perhaps pursue it to a point beyond what Lee himself might have anticipated. Although Jonathan Bate, in his recent *Shakespeare and Ovid,* displays no particular interest in Lee's essay, he does helpfully remark that Arthur Golding's dedicatory epistle to his patron, the Earl of Leicester, expresses the hope that Ovid's "dark Philosophie of turned shapes" might be reconciled with Christian doctrine (Bate, 30). How exactly the doctrine of return might be reconciled Golding does not say. With perhaps more truth than exaggeration, we might say that Shakespeare's oeuvre is constituted in the difference between Ovid's "dark Philosophie" of time and Christian theological tradition. Less ambitiously for the moment, we might note simply the tone of Golding's translation of those lines in book 15 that culminate with Ovid's image of the eternal recurrence of the *cunctus* or total cycle: "the whole round of motion is gone through again" (*novantur*). Here is Golding's Ovid:

In all the world there is not that that standeth at a stay.
Things eb and flow: and every shape is made to passe away.
The tyme itself continually is fleeting like a brooke.
For neyther brooks nor lyghtsome tyme can tarrye still. But looke
As every wave dryves other foorth, and that that comes behynd

Bothe thrusteth and is thrust itself: even so the tymes by kynd
Do fly and follow bothe at once, and evermore renew.

Golding's curious decision to turn the "river" (*flumen*) (on which
Ovid puns prodigiously throughout this passage in the original) to
"brook" because he needs the rhyme scheme has the inadvertent effect
of trivializing the cosmological sublime that governs Pythagoras's
rhetoric. Although Golding's translation may well be, as Ezra Pound
famously remarked, "the most beautiful book in the [English] language," it was doubtless from Ovid himself that Shakespeare came to
recognize that the somewhat vague sense of "evermore renew" in fact
portended the renovation of the absolute cosmos.

   Lee speculated that "the key to the riddle" of the Sonnets lies in the
"philosophic digression in the last book of Ovid's *Metamorphoses*."
Lee's concluding remarks on the effect on Shakespeare of "Ovid's
cyclical creed" is worth citing at length:

The philosophical reflections which pervade [the Sonnets] offer the plain-
est evidence that has yet been adduced of the pagan tone of the poet's voice.
The doctrine that, in spite of all appearances to the contrary, Time is an
endless rotatory process, and that what seems "new" is mere recurrence of
what has "been before," is fatal to all Christian conceptions of the beginning
and end of the world, with its special creations at the outset and its day of
judgement at the close. No notion of the soul's immortality is quite consistent with the cyclical workings of Time and Nature. There is no possibility
of reconciling these cosmic views with Christianity. Such a conclusion is of
importance because it brings Shakespeare's spirit into closer kinship with
the intellectual development of the European Renaissance than is sometimes acknowledged. (Lee, "Ovid and Shakespeare Sonnets," 138–39)

Lee does not assimilate Shakespeare's position to that of Ovid but preserves a careful distinction: "Ovid's creed is that 'revolution' *is* 'the
same,' and that things and their appearances are constantly returning to the same point whence they have come. Shakespeare, although
tempted to assent, stays hesitatingly at the threshold" (132). This seems
to me exactly right, and what I hope to do in the remainder of this

chapter is to articulate Shakespeare's carefully differentiated position more clearly and, above all, to link the idioms of Shakespeare's effort to think the meaning of time to the medieval theological notion of the *aevum*, which is curiously situated between time and eternity, a kind of infinite time that remains quite distinct from *tempus* and *aeternitas*. Once again we are back to the question of the world-historical importance of the translations of *aion* and *eón*, which seem, as always, to lie near the heart of the philosophic and poetic effort to posit the discourses of the highest value: those that presume to lay down the law of time, and to say the name of the most enduring mode of presence.

For Shakespeare proceeds by constantly conjoining the idea of the infinite finitude of an eternally recurring cosmos *and* the idea that there is a constant, unchanging reality somewhere behind or beyond the world of becoming. The fundamental opposition in Shakespeare's thinking is not between reality and appearance, but between a world of irreducible and necessary semblance, namely, eternal return, and a world divided between appearances and a still hidden essence, a world haunted by the possibility that the human spirit might be more than an accident. Shakespeare situates himself in the disjointed differences between these worldviews. To come to believe in eternal return à la Ovid and the Dionysian cults would be once again to resort to metaphysics, regardless of how ironic or melancholy one's belief may be. Lee states the case for a materialist metaphysics: "The universe of matter is, on Ovid's hypothesis, an ever-turning wheel, which suffers nothing to be either new or old; the appearances of constant change or innovation are due to the effect of a regularly gyrating recurrence" (126). Shakespeare, however, is too modern and thus entirely aware that the all too obviously narcissistic desire for infinite time, whether as recurrent becoming or hypostatic infinite duration, is in both instances an effort to foreclose the possibility that the cosmos may be a singular event without possibility of return and without relation to any realm of value or Being.

Let us begin by reading sonnets 59 and 60 because they explicitly rework and retranslate Ovid's theses on time. Shakespeare's topic at this point is the curious resistance the young man seems to enjoy vis-à-vis the passage of time, which seems to afflict everyone but him. And so, the admiring poet wonders in sonnet 59 whether there might be any precedents in the ancient world for such extraordinary beauty:

If there be nothing new, but that which is
Hath been before, how are our brains beguiled,
Which, labouring for invention, bear amiss
The second burden of a former child!
O that record could with a backward look
Even of five hundred courses of the sun
Show me your image in some antique book
Since mind at first in character was done,
That I might see what the old world could say
To this composèd wonder of your frame;
Whether we are mended or whe'er better they,
Or whether revolution be the same.

      O, sure I am the wits of former days
      To subjects worse have given admiring praise.

I want to suggest that the most significant thing about this sonnet is not its indecision with respect to the question of whether human history progresses, regresses, or stays the same, but its somewhat enigmatic allusion to giving birth a second time to the same child. What "antique" image in "the old world" could Shakespeare be thinking of in connection with this "second burden of a former child" who in effect has already transformed every apparent act of invention into an unwitting repetition?

Of the many editions of the Sonnets I have consulted, I have never found an editor willing even to speculate on what may lie behind Shakespeare's singular image of the double birth. Stephen Booth and John Kerrigan allude to the idea that "five hundred courses of the sun" may allude to "the Great Year" (Booth, 237; Kerrigan, 247), but it is very unlikely that Shakespeare could have believed (even poetically) that the cosmos completed its rotary cycle in so brief a time, and the phrase more likely refers simply to an amount of time that would allow any changes in human beauty to become discernible. While several editors and students of sonnets 59 and 60 have noted their echoes of book 15 of the *Metamorphoses,* no one appears to have remarked the connection of "the second burden" to the birth of Bacchus, which Ovid recounts in book 3. Semele, who is pregnant with Bacchus, asks Jove to appear to her: "Her mortal body bore not the onrush of heavenly power, and by that gift of wedlock she was consumed. The babe still not wholly fashioned is snatched from the mother's womb and (if report may be believed) sewed up in his father's thigh, there to await its full time of birth" (3:308–12). Because "the second burden of a former child" has thus far received no commentary of any sort, the suggestion that Dionysus/Bacchus is the secret name, the improper proper name, of that innermost experience of time is likely to appear somewhat jarring and productive of more than a little resistance. Shakespeare would also have known that Bacchus/Liber was for Ovid the god of "the innermost presence," or in Shakespeare's idiom, that which beguiles the brain at the very heart of the labor of invention, the name of the (possibly) abyssal aporia of time and thought, and even of poetry itself. In Shakespeare's encounter with the thought of eternal recurrence a Pythagorean-Heraclitean cosmology is once again articulated around the figure of Dionysus.

Like a psychoanalyst, Prospero urges Miranda to recollect her past before coming to the island: "What seest thou else / In the dark backward and abysme of time?" (*The Tempest* 1.2.49–50). In a similar vein we might adduce Hamlet's famous remark to the gravedigger as he unearths decomposed human remains from burials long past: "Here's fine revolution, an we had the trick to see't" (5.1.83–84). But let us consider more closely the nature of this "fine revolution" and "the trick" that might help us understand it better. As the clown disinters one skull after another, Hamlet has quite a clear image of what this circulation of bones might be about: "Did these bones cost no more the breeding but to play at loggats with 'em. Mine ache to think on't" (84–85). Loggats are, as the word suggests, little sticks, which are thrown at a stake in the ground in a game that resembles horseshoes. Hamlet's point is unmistakable: our bones are bred and scattered in this "fine revolution," in this infinite circulation of life and death, with as little regard as though they were inanimate pieces in a child's game. Is it not apparent? Hamlet's macabre vision of life as a charnel house is simply another version of Heraclitean Aion playing with time and Being like a child playing draughts.

The closer we look, the more pervasive and relentless Shakespeare's questioning of the aporia of time appears. At the gateway of abysmal time many forms and shapes come to presence before Shakespeare's imagination. Some are quite terrible, while others, like the young man who is "the master-mistress of my passion" (sonnet 20), are "beguiling." Before considering sonnet 60, we might anticipate for a moment our discussion of Nietzsche and mention a draft of a poem in his notebooks for 1882–83 called "Yorick-Columbus," in which Hamlet, gazing at Yorick's skull and into the abysmal revolutions or cycles of time, comes to resemble Columbus's discovery of new worlds. Although Nietzsche rarely openly acknowledges a debt to Shakespeare as an important precursor in the secret history of eternal recurrence, and this despite the fact that Nietzsche's thinking about eternal return is everywhere colored by Shakespeare's phrasings, the mere connection of Yorick and Columbus is homage enough. The only thing really notable about the poem, other than its title, is its concluding line, in which Nietzsche celebrates the strange beauty that is the aporia of time: "the most beautiful monstrosity: eternity [*Ewigkeit*]" (*KSA* 11:328). The Medusalike monstrosity of eternity is not only beautiful but "the most beautiful." We will return later to Nietzsche's embrace of the Medusa as the very soul of the Dionysian; for now our concern is with Shakespeare's very similar experience.

Here is sonnet 60:

Like as the waves make towards the pebbled shore,
So do our minutes hasten to their end,
Each changing place with that which goes before;
In sequent toil all forwards do contend.
Nativity, once in the main of light,
Crawls to maturity, wherewith being crowned
Crookèd eclipses 'gainst his glory fight,
And time that gave doth now his gift confound.
Time doth transfix the flourish set on youth,

And delves the parallels in beauty's brow;
Feeds on the rarities of nature's truth,
And nothing stands but for his scythe to mow.
        And yet to times in hope my verse shall stand,
        Praising thy worth despite his cruel hand.

Time's assault on youth will, however, prove strangely ineffective on the young man, who, as we will see, soon appears impervious to time's onslaughts. The curious expression, unique in Shakespeare, that "Time doth transfix the flourish set on youth," is actually quite consistent with the notion of time's incessant movement, for it suggests that what time has "set" or fixed or imprinted on human youth and beauty will in time be removed as youth crescendos in maturity and begins its long decline. To "transfix" would thus in this context have the sense of "changing place with that which goes before," which is to say that time repeatedly re-fixes or resets "the flourish" on other youthful beauties as it transfixes it from those who pass on to maturity.

Much of Shakespeare's argument in the Sonnets to this point has been concerned with urging the young man to breed offspring as a way of vying with time, and, alternately, with the work of poetry itself as a means of securing his eternal fame:

And all in war with Time for love of you,
As he takes from you, I ingraft you new. (sonnet 15)

All of which transpires on "this huge stage" where the "stars in secret influence" regulate the entire cycle of giving the gift and confounding it. On the one hand, the poet's innermost sense of his calling is that of somehow circumventing or delaying the otherwise irresistible prospect of being "sunk in hideous night" (#12) or lost in "death's eternal cold" (#13). Given his apparent refusal to procreate, the young man's "eternal summer" seems at this early point still to depend entirely on the poet's "eternal lines" if he is to enjoy the maximum duration as a living form, not a separate or individual consciousness but rather a particular physical form that stands at the zenith of youthful beauty:

Nor shall death brag thou wander'st in his shade
When in eternal lines to time thou grow'st.

So long as men can breathe or eyes can see,
So long lives this, and this gives life to thee. (#18)

The young man is of course at once inseparable from and irreducible to a singular biographical identity, which is to say he is and is not an actor, as Oscar Wilde would have it, a patron, or an amalgam of features of several actors and patrons. However, he is above all a figure of the point at which thinking confronts the incontrovertible aporia that lies at the conjunction of the question of time and the duration of human history.

Although thought "can't leap large lengths" (#44), and any speculations are to be regarded with caution, the poet assimilates the young man to a necessary moment of good fortune in a world ruled by chance that must eternally recur: "you in every blessèd shape we know have some part" (#53). While time the devourer of all things consumes us insofar as we consume ourselves (cf. sonnets 1 and 2), the beauty of the young man, in conjunction with the poet's art, can actually succeed in slowing this process down: "Give my love fame faster than time wastes life" (#100). In order to slow "time's thievish progress to eternity" (#77), the poet must spend his life in the effort of fending off time through a certain perfection of language. That is why the passing reflection on eternal return in sonnets 59 and 60 is finally a somewhat consoling thought, since here, if only hypothetically, we have a principle of the conservation of energy that preserves identity from cycle to cycle.

Things begin to shift more decisively in sonnet 67, where the young man's natural gifts of beauty are now seen to surpass any aesthetic "false painting," which means that art's impoverishment vis-à-vis nature has become irrefutable: "For she [nature] hath no exchequer now but his." He has become, in other words, the sign in nature that something in nature survives, that somehow the energy and matter and form are preserved so that this extraordinary, apparently altogether exceptional beauty should itself be the cipher of an immeasurable structure of restitution and replication, a force, which is Time itself, that can and does "copy" and "print more" (11). Herein lies the antinomical structure of the aporia of time in the Sonnets, for although

poetry appears to be at war with time, the inner form of this osten-
sible war is actually the secret affirmation of time as eternal return;
the only war is the war that is incessantly raging within time itself, and
that is what ensures the reproduction and revolution of the same. The
poet perishes but not without the faint hope that the young man's apparent resistance to time, his ability somehow to break or suspend the
onrushing of time, might stand as a cipher, an allegory for the eternal
return of the total cycle. His beauty is the trace of some still enigmatic
disjunction within the presence of the present, the thought of ontological difference and the recognition that nothing of Being's essence
makes its way to beings but the difference (or war with time) itself.
The war between poetry or life and Time the destroyer is finally a mis-
leading abstraction that fails to attend closely enough to the realm of
appearance. Rather than assuming that some realm of higher value
and a more authentic modality of existence lies somewhere behind or
beyond the world of mere becoming, the task of poetic thinking in the
Sonnets is that of affirming the possibility of the survival of absolute
recurrent beauty through "death's dateless night" (#30).

Let us conclude this brief discussion of the Sonnets by looking at
sonnet 68 and its macabre allegory of the golden fleece, which we will
link to *The Merchant of Venice* before turning to other plays and issues:

Thus is his cheek the map of days outworn,
When beauty lived and died as flowers do now,
Before these bastard signs of fair were borne
Or durst inhabit on a living brow;
Before the golden tresses of the dead,
The right of sepulchres, were shorn away
To live a second life on second head;
Ere beauty's dead fleece made another gay.
In him those holy antique hours are seen
Without all ornament, itself and true,
Making no summer of another's green,
Robbing no old to dress his beauty new;
　　And him as for a map doth nature store,
　　To show false art what beauty was of yore.

The young man's circumvention of time is nowhere more apparent in the Sonnets than here, where his cheek never needs makeup, his hair retains all its beauty, and thus he has no need of some corpse's beautiful "dead fleece" to cover his baldness, and where we bear witness to the presence in him of "those holy antique hours" that presumably lead all the way back to nature's beginnings. The young man is, in effect, the cipher of true time, the trace or promise in the realm of appearance, in the visual phenomenal world, of the irreducibility of the world of becoming. That he ages so much more slowly, that he seems unchanged when the poet himself has been ravaged by time and care, may be the sign of nature's formidable "store" as a reservoir of time that endows the finite manifestation of the young man's beauty with a kind of infinity over the long term.

   This sonnet is closely linked to Bassanio's rumination in *The Merchant of Venice* over which of the three caskets to choose in order to win Portia's hand:

> Look on beauty
> And you shall see 'tis purchased by the weight,
> Which wherein works a miracle in nature,
> Making them lightest that wear most of it.
> So are those crispèd, snaky, golden locks
> Which makes such wanton gambols with the wind
> Upon supposèd fairness, often known
> To be the dowry of a second head,
> The skull that bred them in the sepulchre.
> Thus ornament is but the guilèd shore
> To a most dangerous sea, the beauteous scarf
> Veiling an Indian beauty; in a word,
> The seeming truth which cunning times put on
> To entrap the wisest. (3.2.88–101)

Although he appears to be thinking about the difference between the gold, the silver, and the lead caskets, Bassanio is really thinking about Portia's astonishing locks, whose spiderlike and luxuriant embroidery are very much a part of his desire for her ("A golden mesh t'untrap the hearts of men" [122]). The larger point of course is that appearances are in fact highly revealing once one looks into them, and the natural living beauty will always outshine even those "miracle[s] in nature" which art, including the art of wig making, can forge. Thus Portia's living fleece is implicitly being contrasted with the most beguiling and Medusalike wig. That Portia will later don the dead fleece of a judge's wig in her dispensation of justice to Shylock is vaguely anticipated here; but more important is certainly Bassanio's irrepressible delight in "those crispèd, snaky, golden locks" that belie the seductive extremities which "cunning times" do not hesitate to exploit.

Shakespeare imagines a love not "subject to time's love or to time's hate," which is to say a relation to the young man's beauty that is "builded far from accident" (#124). We must learn to negotiate Shakespeare's idea that love is not prey to time through the protocols of the doctrine of return, which means that, from cycle to cycle, the relation of love "is an ever fixèd mark" (#116), and that the only meaningful sense in which love is not "time's fool" (#116; or #124 "the fools of time") is that love knows that time itself is irreducible. Although there is much that is transfixed (or erased) as one passes through time, there is also an element of sameness and fixity within the world of becoming itself. At the same time, however, Shakespeare clearly wants to situate this world of fixity not within the world of accident but far from it. And yet Shakespeare says that love endures "even to the edge of doom" (#116) not "beyond" it or "through" it. And since time itself bears itself out "even to the edge of doom," the implicit contrast is mute and contradictory in precisely the same economy that Bassanio's opposition of Portia's locks to the Medusa locks of the dead fleece was itself reversible. "Sacred beauty" offers not an escape from but an affirmation of the inescapability of "time's tyranny" (#115).

But let us continue for a moment on the topic of periwigs and the baldness of Old Father Time, and on the way wigs try to cover up the fact that we finally cannot conceal our radical nonknowledge of time and cannot step beyond the antinomy of time. If one could be sure that love survived the judgments of time and the intervals of cosmic recycling, then one would effectively be able to seize Time by the forelock, and many Shakespearean persona try mightily to do so. Let us consider a comic (but very serious) set of incidents in that veritable critique of the metaphysics of morals, *The Comedy of Errors.* Just as the confusions are beginning to unfold between the Ephesian Antipholus, his serving man Dromio, and their Syracusan doubles, the latter pair, newly arrived amid the apparent enchantments of Ephesus, begin to reflect on whether something has happened to time:

ANTIPHOLUS OF SYRACUSE. Well, sir, learn to jest in good time. There's a
   time for all things.
DROMIO OF SYRACUSE. [who has just been beaten by Antipholus of Ephe-
   sus] I durst have denied that before you were so choleric.
ANTIPHLOUS OF SYRACUSE. By what rule, sir?
DROMIO OF SYRACUSE. Marry, sir, by a rule as plain as the plain bald pate
   of Father Time himself.
ANTIPHOLUS OF SYRACUSE. Let's hear it.
DROMIO OF SYRACUSE. There's no time for a man to recover his hair that
   grows bald by nature.
ANTIPHLOUS OF SYRACUSE. May he not do it by fine and recovery?
DROMIO OF SYRACUSE. Yes, to pay a fine for a periwig, and recover the lost
   hair of another man.
ANTIPHOLUS OF SYRACUSE. Why is Time such a niggard of hair, being, as
   it is, so plentiful in excrement? (2.2.63–78)

Dromio goes on to remark that man's scant hair and wit are in contrast to the plentiful growth that animals enjoy. Antipholus concludes
that Dromio has "proved there is no time for all things" (101), which is
to say, as Dromio replies, "no time to recover hair lost by nature":

ANTIPHOLUS OF SYRACUSE. But your reason was not substantial, why there
   is no time to recover.
DROMIO OF SYRACUSE. Thus I mend it: Time himself is bald, and therefore
   to the world's end will have bald followers.
ANTIPHOLUS OF SYRACUSE. I knew 'twould be a bald conclusion. (104–8)

Shakespeare's recurrent association of periwigs with the antinomies
of time constitutes one of the most striking time-fetishes in world
literature. Whether or not we will have hair when our bodies are resurrected, or for that matter teeth, or good digestion, is a perennial

question with respect to the Christian mysteries of resurrection in Pauline Ephesus. Whether we recover our hair in a spiritual afterlife of the disembodied body, or whether the world of becoming is replayed over again is what is really at issue in *The Comedy of Errors*. Even the sexual imbroglios between wives and mistresses, lovers and servants have significance for the aporias of time, particularly in connection with the kitchen wench whose amorous nature has become alarmingly apparent to the Syracusan Dromio:

Marry, sir, she's the kitchen wench, and all grease; and I know not what use to put her to but to make a lamp of her, and run from her by her own light. I warrant her rags and the tallow in them will burn a Poland winter. If she lives till doomsday, she'll burn a week longer than the whole world. (3.2.94–99)

The possibility of the survival of the world of becoming after dooms-day is synonymous with eternal return, and thus with another mode of recovery and survival. But since there are only "bald conclusions" and scant proofs, the only material remnant we have to base our thoughts about time upon is really the dead fleece; in which case the Christian resurrection and life everlasting and the melancholy ironies of eternal recurrence appear only as rival manufacturers of fetish corpse excrements.

All of which inevitably makes us "the fools of time" and subject to "time's tyranny." In this connection Richard C. McCoy's recent reading of Shakespeare's "The Phoenix and Turtle," which was published in 1601, just after the execution of the Earl of Essex, seems to me to hit the right tone with respect to Shakespeare's sense of Christian resurrection in particular and in general the expectation that human existence should be more than an accident of time and nature. Written at what must doubtless have been a low point in Shakespeare's expectations about the fate of England, "The Phoenix and Turtle" is an ironic lyric meditation on a phoenix who is not self-resurrecting:

Death is now the phoenix's nest,
And the turtle's loyal breast
To eternity doth rest.

. . .

Truth may seem but cannot be,
Beauty brag, but 'tis not she.
Truth and beauty buried be.

Truth and beauty rather than Essex and Queen Elizabeth are at issue here. The poem concludes with Shakespeare's request that we "sigh a prayer" before the urn where they "enclosed in cinders lie." "Death is now the phoenix's nest," but what about later; is it not possible, since "Beauty, truth, and rarity, / Grace in all simplicity, / Here enclosed in cinders lie," that these entities might arise into the world of becoming once again? Here is McCoy's observation:

> There is finally no "sure and certain hope of resurrection" [Book of Common Prayer] for love's martyrs in Shakespeare. His vision of human sacrifice in both the love poetry and the sonnets has its eucharistic aspects, but neither "The Phoenix and Turtle" nor the sacrificial sonnets [nos. 124–136] are truly sacramental. What we get instead of a real presence or holy communion are "dead birds" and "fools of time." Yet these poetic renderings remain sacred objects of a sort, not sacraments but relics. (McCoy, "Love's Martyrs," 302)

Like those Nietzschean and Derridean "cinders" which we will consider in chapter 7, these Shakespearean cinders are strangely lodged between an absolute irony and a faintly ironic hope. The involutions of Shakespeare's war with time are perhaps best characterized by Walter Benjamin when he observes of the *Trauerspiel* tradition of allegory that the vile and lowly things it adduces as evidence of the insignificance of human existence, like ashes, corpses, and specters, also possess a secret allegorical dimension that holds open the promise of eternal life (of some sort) at the very moment it would appear to be closed absolutely:

And this is the essence of melancholy immersion: that its ultimate objects, in which it believes it can most fully secure for itself that which is vile, turn into allegories, and that these allegories fill out and deny the void in which they are represented, just as, ultimately, the intention does not faithfully rest in the contemplation of bones, but faithlessly leaps forward to the idea of resurrection [*zur Auferstehung treulos überspringt*] (*The Origin of German Tragic Drama*, 232–33).

And it is exactly this faithless leap that affirms life and compels it onward; and this could not be otherwise even though what awaits us is an infinite expanse of nonbeing. Shakespeare's cinder relics lie near the center of what is most particular to his historical experience of the aporia of time.

Moreover, they import, if not a messianic impulse, then at least what Derrida calls a certain "messianicity," an affirmation of the little knowledge they possess and of the larger secret in which all of human history still appears to Shakespeare to be suspended. To give an even later instance of Shakespeare's Baroque sense of a suppressed messianic hope of a revelation to come, we might adduce *The Two Noble Kinsmen* and Palamon's prayer to Venus, "the sovereign queen of secrets" (5.2.9), but above all the play's overall stoic acceptance of a world of ceaseless change whose gods, like Arcite's "heavenly limiter" (5.1.29), make us into things we cannot identify or understand. As Theseus says, in what may be some of Shakespeare's very last words for the stage:

What things you make of us! For what we lack
We laugh, for what we have, are sorry; still
Are children in some kind. Let us be thankful
For that which is, and with you leave dispute
That are above our question. Let's go off
And bear us like the time. (5.6.131–37)

4

Anamorphic Perspectives, Human (Im)postures,

and the Rhetoric of the *Aevum*

Eternity, of course, was God's timeless and motionless Now-and-Ever, knowing neither past nor future. *Aevum,* however, was a kind of infiniteness and duration which had motion and therefore past and future, a sempiternity which according to all authorities was endless. There was difference of opinion though, whether that sempiternity, which was created, was created before Time or together with Time; that is to say, whether *aevum* was infinite only in view of the future or also in view of the past. ERNST KANTOROWICZ, *The King's Two Bodies*

My effort to situate the aesthetic, rhetorical, and political status of Shakespeare's time-fetishes is organized around the notions of anamorphosis and the Tudor idea of the sovereign's *corpus mysticus,* which will help us understand the ironic position of Shakespeare's manipulation of the fetish-image vis-à-vis the political theology of his era. It is the life of the institution of kingship rather than its abstract eternal divinity that most interested the apologists of the Tudor state, who justified the new regime on the notion of the perpetuity of the very idea of the state above and beyond the life of its members or even its sovereigns. As a mere adducement of a divine *parousia* or manifestation, the *corpus mysticus* had no doubt lost much of its ancient appeal by the mid-sixteenth century (cf. David Norbrook, "The Emperor's New Body?"). What Ernst Kantorowicz demonstrated, however, was the genealogy through which "the fiction of a quasi-infinite continuity of public institutions" could have been invented (*The King's*

Two Bodies, 284). As Edmund Plowden remarked in his *Treatise of the Two Bodies of the King, viz. Natural and Politic,* the very idea of the body politic was a kind of affirmation of life, a sublime but necessary fiction "constituted and devysed by reason and pollicy and of mere necessitie for preservation of the people" (cited in Marie Axton, *The Queen's Two Bodies,* 28).

As we can see from Kantorowicz's account, the late medieval theology of the *aevum,* of an ontological region in the difference between *aion* and *tempus,* simply formalizes and gives a name to the long-standing instability in the history of philosophy between the eternal and what lives eternally. The *aevum* is an angelic realm between God and mortals, whose denizens live throughout infinite time but who were created by God and are thus not co-eternal with Him:

> But the immortal spirits had a share also in terrestrial Time, not only because they could appear to men within Time, but also because they were created and therefore had, after their peculiar angelic fashion, a Before and an After. *Aevum* (in fact a far more complicated notion than can be demonstrated here), bridged the chasm between timeless Eternity and finite Time. If God in his Eternity was the Immutable beyond and without Time, and if man in his *tempus* was the Mutable within a mutable and changing finite Time, then the angels were the Immutable within a changing, though infinite, *aevum.* (Kantorowicz, *The King's Two Bodies,* 280–81)

We might generalize and say that the notion of the body politic, which emerged in connection with the monarch's *corpus mysticus* and was later appropriated as a description of a free association of citizens in the political space of the state, remains in all its forms the effort to define the nature of power in terms of a certain relation between time and eternity. Kantorowicz does not recognize the obvious signs here of a return of the idea of eternal return in the very notion of the *aevum,* which also signals a return to a more material manifestation of the meaning of *aion.* The life of the state, of its power, of the power of a people to be thus constituted, all these issues emerge at the moment when the ideologeme of the *corpus mysticus* is negated at one level, since we see, with Hamlet, the perfidy of Claudius, who is the hypocritical arch-defender of the old pieties, and yet this archaic notion of the mystical body of power is preserved at another level, since we see, again through Hamlet's eyes, the way a fawning court blindly pays homage to the trappings of power with which a murderer has dressed himself. We see that, although the king is a thing of nothing, nevertheless this "nothing" organizes the forms and expressions of power.

Shakespeare could have gleaned the notion of "the mystical foundations of authority" from other sources than Montaigne, but since he knew Montaigne's writing so well, we might attend to an interesting passage in one of the later essays, "De l'incommodité de la grandeur" [The Incommodity of Greatness] (trans. Florio), or "On High Rank as a Disadvantage" (trans. Screech); here is Screech's version:

> This kingly quality stifles and annihilates their other qualities, their real ones which are of their essence: they lie buried under their royal state. That leaves them with no means of showing their worth except actions which directly touch upon their royal state or which contribute to it, namely the duties of their rank. Which means that such a one is so entirely a king that he has no other existence. That radiance which surrounds him is not him, but it hides and conceals him from us: the rays from our eyes strike against it and are scattered, being overwhelmed and arrested by the strong light. [*Cette lueuer estrange qui l'environne, le cache et nous le desrobe, nostre veuë s'y rompt et s'y dissipe, estant remplie et arrestée par cette lumière.*] (*Complete Essays*, 1042; *Essais*, 3:15)

Here is the last sentence in Florio's version:

> That strange glimmering and eye-dazeling light, which round about environeth, overcasteth and hideth from us: our weake sight is thereby bleared and dissipated, as beeing [*sic*] filled and obscured by that greater and further-spredding brightnesse. (*Essays*, 3:155)

Hamlet, of course, suspects that the mystical foundations of the early modern experience of the royal person are "more than natural":

> It is not strange; for mine uncle is King of Denmark, and those that would make mows [grimaces] at him while my father lived give twenty, forty, an hundred ducats apiece for his picture in little. 'Sblood, there is something in this more than natural, if philosophy could find it out. (2.2.347–51)

Screech's somewhat excessive rendering of *estrange lueuer* as a radi-ance that "surrounds him [but] is not him" does, however, point us in the right direction, since power cannot be seen clearly but only in a bleared, distorted image. Furthermore, the royal auratic radiance is at once expressive of the abyssal character of power and authority and yet it still remains a narcissistic projection on the part of individuals who need to feel they must have some connection to a quasi-eternal order of Being. We want to believe that we are the beings of Being, while Shakespeare is intent on showing us that our notion of Being has no relation to anything that might really be out there but is instead a notion of Being wholly of and for beings. Like Montaigne, he sees the aura of kingship simply as an encumbrance that obstructs the king in his own efforts to take stock of his real responsibilities. Montaigne's point, and often Shakespeare's as well, is that the monarch himself risks being overwhelmed by his aura no less than do his subjects.

Kantorowicz credits Shakespeare's *Richard II* with having decisively undermined the myth of the divine fullness of the royal presence (*The Kings's Two Bodies*, 24–41). Kantorowicz adduces the shattered mirror and the deposition scene as the focal points, but he never mentions the pervasively anamorphic imagery of the play overall. What I want to argue is that, while the temporality of the *aevum* made conceptu-ally and imaginatively available to Shakespeare a new, realistic notion of kingship and sovereignity based on fortune and the randomness of destiny, when it came to visualizing this new (but, as it happens, very ancient) notion of infinite time, it was to the technique of anamorphic painting that Shakespeare turned in order to describe or dramatize the emergence into our visual field of the temporality of the *aevum*. Before the aporia of time, Shakespeare asks us to envision anamorphic per-spectives, carefully calculated distortions that cause the world of ap-pearance and becoming to shake, to slow down, to break the rhythm of experience. In this caesura or suspensive moment we glimpse un-canny or terrible perspectives on the future, or surpassingly beautiful images of desire. Shakespeare's anamorphic time-fetishes are images not of eternity but of the infinite time of the *aevum*.

But before sketching the history of anamorphic art during the later sixteenth century, let us return to *Richard II* and to the corrupt and decadent courtier, Bushy's allusion to anamorphic art with which he tries to calm the distraught queen by explaining that her premonition that Richard's departure portends a world of grief is merely the result of an optical illusion, since her tears altered her focus, which thus

Divides one thing entire to many objects,
Like perspectives, which rightly gazed upon,
Show nothing but confusion—eyed awry,
Distinguish form. (2.2.17–20)

"Divides" here means "spreads out," smears or blears, the image after the fashion of an anamorphic portrait which distorts facial features into almost unrecognizable shape. Bushy continues:

So your sweet majesty
Looking awry upon your lord's departure,
Finds shapes of grief more than himself to wail
Which, looked on as it is, is naught but shadows
Of what is not. (20–24)

Bushy is trying to dissuade the queen from believing that she has seen the shape of the future. What is at stake, in other words, is not so much looking at the king or looking through tears, as it is trying to look into time itself, which of course cannot be done and which leads invariably to the aporia of time. Here the aporia takes the form of antinomical meanings of "to eye awry," which in Bushy's first usage seems to mean that to eye something awry is to begin to see things clearly (i.e., "Distinguish form"), albeit not by looking at something straight on (i.e., "rightly"), but rather by gazing at an angle, askance, which conforms to the convention of viewing an anamorphic perspective from a viewing screen set up at an oblique angle and calculated to present the only clearly focused perspective on the image, which, if viewed from any other angle, appeared distorted; Bushy's second usage, "Looking awry," entirely reverses the sense of the first usage and insists, quite paradoxically, on using "Looking awry" as though it meant precisely the opposite of "eyed awry"! "Awry" thus ends up meaning two contradictory things in Bushy's semantics: (1) looking aslant and thus rightly focused, and (2) looking aslant and thus seeing things that do not exist. Bushy's overheated rhetoric is of a piece with the penchant of Richard's court for excess and subterfuge. Richard himself continues this merely obfuscating use of the language of anamorphosis when he accuses Bolingbroke and the conspirators of being "marked with a blot" for their disloyalty (4.1.226). But while Bushy and Richard are unabashedly proud of their criminal abuse of power, and while they use the fashionable language of anamorphosis to mislead others, Isabella's anamorphic vision of "Some unborn sorrow, ripe in fortune's womb" coming toward her (2.2.10–11) accurately anticipates the judgment that is to come. Anamorphic perspectives do not function in Shakespeare as the vehicles of some sort of undecidable and irreducible confusion but, quite to the contrary, as apparatuses for distinguishing the aporia of time from what can be known and judged.

Although anamorphic painting and drawing were widely practiced throughout the period from Leonardo da Vinci to Albrecht Dürer, the technique did not come into vogue in the courts of Europe until the 1520s and 1530s. William (or Guillim) Scrots was hired at an unprecedented salary to replace Hans Holbein as the king's painter in the court of Henry VIII in 1546. Ellis Waterhouse has remarked that "although Scrots was not a painter of high creative or imaginative gifts, he knew all the latest fashions, and a series of portraits appeared at the English Court during the next few years which could vie in modernity with those produced anywhere in northern Europe, even by painters of much greater natural distinction" (Waterhouse, *Painting in Britain*, 24; cf. Strong, *Tudor and Jacobean Portraits*, 87–89; and Kemp, *The Science of Art*, 208–12). Scrots's famous anamorphic portrait of Edward VI (now in the National Portrait Gallery, London) was exhibited at Whitehall Palace during the winter of 1591–92, when Shakespeare and his company played there. Allan Shickman has remarked on the sensation created by this painting at Whitehall: "Court visitors to Whitehall often mentioned this anamorphosis in their journals. Apparently, every guest of any importance was taken to see it, and Shakespeare was doubtless no exception" (Shickman, " 'Turning Pictures,' " 67). Shickman, however, believes that Scrots's elongated ana-

c portrait of the young king was not in Shakespeare's thoughts
ard II, which Shickman believes refers to the practice of "the
ig or pleated picture," which is a technique of painting two
ings, one on each side of a louvered or pleated vertical panel
h constitutes the painting's surface. Thus, two completely differ-
images appear depending on whether one views the picture from
right or the left. Shickman borrows the expression "turning pic-
re" from Burton's *Anatomy of Melancholy* (1621), which refers to a
icture that depicts both a fair maid and an ape; and Shakespeare
is clearly thinking of this device in the famous "natural perspective"
of *Twelfth Night,* which we will examine in a moment, as well as the
alternating figures of Mars and a Gorgon in *Antony and Cleopatra*
and *Romeo and Juliet*'s anamorphic swan and crow. There is a striking pleated anamorphosis of Mary, Queen of Scots and a death's head
in the Scottish National Portrait Gallery in Edinburgh. Since there appears to be little consensus on this issue, it may be important to note
that, pace Shickman, *Richard II* is unquestionably a kind of homage
to Scrots's portrait of Edward, where rather than two discrete images
we see "nothing but confusion."

Shakespeare appears to have considered closely the implications of
the anamorphic styles that were, luckily for him, revived from the
1530s just in time to make an impact on his mature vision of art's
perspective on time. And like Elizabeth's court during the nineties,
the court of Henri IV in France was also caught up in the anamorphic vogue. Ellis Waterhouse has suggested that anamorphic portrai-
ture was "especially used for the furtherance of political propaganda
abroad" (26). R. J. W. Evans speculates that the wavering of the subject in anamorphic art is to be understood against the backdrop of a
shift in power on the Continent that saw the decline of the Hapsburg
court and the ascendancy of French and British interests (Evans, "The
Imperial Court in the Time of Archimboldo"). In addition to the two
forms of anamorphic art to which Shakespeare repeatedly refers, there
was also a very popular tradition of calculating the distortions of the
anamorphic portrait so that the image could be seen clearly only when
reflected on a conical mirror or reflective surface that was placed at

the center of the image (and thus served as a kind of viewing screen).
As sophisticated visual calling-cards, anamorphic portraits were the
vague equivalent of a sixteenth-century high-tech commercial.

Scrots's portrait of Edward followed Holbein's famous "Ambassadors" (1533) and contemporaneous anamorphic portraits of Charles V,
François I, Ferdinand I, and Pope Paul II. Scrots's other portraits,
including those of Princess Elizabeth (1547) and the ill-fated Henry
Howard, Earl of Surrey (1546), are very strikingly evocative of a singular moment, but they are not anamorphic. This should give us a sense
of what made anamorphosis so appealing to the sixteenth-century
artists: its sharp sense of the aesthetics of the singular moment, something not unlike the leap of Titian's Bacchus, a freeze-frame technique
that tries to capture the otherwise concealed nature of time and the
world of becoming precisely by appearing to slow it down, to arrest
duration so that its elementary structure can be made visible. Scrots's
anamorphic portrait of Edward literally stretches the image out of
shape, out of joint, while he depicts the adolescent Elizabeth as though
seized in a particular moment as she stands beside a lectern with an
open book whose pages we can see have just been turned. Likewise,
the poet Surrey gazes into a melancholy void while leaning on a ruined
column, all of which is suspended against an abstract cloudy vacuity.
This is always of course the caesuralike effect of the gaze, its ability
to break the normative illusion of continuous duration and so-called
natural consciousness by holding the subject, as Jacques Lacan puts it,
"suspended in an essential vacillation" (*Four Fundamental Concepts of
Psycho-Analysis,* 83).

In the "Ambassadors," Lacan has remarked, "Holbein makes visible
for us here something that is simply the subject as annihilated," which
means that the anamorphic object, in this case, the smear in the painting's foreground that clearly appears as a death's head only when
viewed from an angle directly beneath the painting, disrupts the subject, divides it, puts it out of joint, through what Lacan calls "the
function of the lack, of the appearance of the phallic ghost" (*Four
Fundamental Concepts,* 89, 88).

Because it involves exactly the sort of detail in Holbein's painting that Scrots, his heir apparent, would have surely noticed, let us

within the time of human history. Imogen asleep at the entrance to the cave, and disguised as Fidelio, appears to onlookers in *Cymbeline* like an "earthly paragon" (3.7.16); and Marina in *Pericles* is "a paragon" formed by nature: "nature fram'd this piece" (4.2.136–37). All the difficulties in the plot of *Cymbeline* stem from Iachimo's somewhat understandable outrage at Posthumous's extravagant praise of Imogen at the expense of Roman women. Imogen herself seems to take exception at Posthumous's "Postures beyond brief nature" (5.5.165), which, although undertaken on her behalf, seem to her hollow and not to be compared to her feelings for him, which, as the play confirms, are of a very different order: "O, not like me: / For mine's beyond beyond" (3.2.56–57), which means *within* the world of becoming and not in some meaningless abstraction. Posthumous's rhetorical postures are impostures.

Man is "the paragon of the animals" who pleases not Hamlet; and "to paragon" is a transitive verb in *Othello*. In these and many other instances Shakespeare is always, in one way or another, situating a presumptive transcendence of becoming back within "brief nature." Shakespeare's ideas and his interest in the "posture" of the paragon seem to me to derive a great deal from Montaigne's ironic treatment of those who suffer from "*une évidente imposture de la veuë*" (*Essais* 3:306), which means "an evident deception of the sight" (trans. Florio, 3:315); "an evident imposture of our sight" (trans. Frame, 449); and that "which shows how sight can deceive us" (trans. Screech, 672). To deceive us, that is, into forgetting that, as Montaigne phrases it, à la Plutarch, "We have no communication with Being" (trans. Screech, 680). This phrase ("*Nous n'avons aucune communication à l'estre*") is itself a translation from Plutarch's essay "Of the Word *EI* Engraved over the Gate of Apollo's Temple at Delphi," which means the word "eternity," *aion, eón*. "With the words '*Present*,' '*This instant*,' '*Now*,' we above all appear," writes Plutarch (cited by Montaigne, trans. Screech, 682), "to support and stabilize our understanding of Time: but Reason strips it bare and at once destroys it: for Reason straightway cleaves *Now* into distinct parts, the future and the past, as needing of necessity to see it thus divided into two parts." Plutarch's God remains alone, inaccessibly beyond "any measure known to Time." To this "very religious conclusion of a pagan," Montaigne opposes the Stoic transcendence of Seneca, who hopes to "rise above humanity" (*s'eleve au dessus de l'humanité*). It is precisely this imposture that Montaigne's pagan Christianity tries to renounce: "Nor may a man mount above himself or above humanity." "It is for our Christian faith," concludes Montaigne, à la Plutarch, and "not that Stoic virtue of [Seneca], to aspire to that holy and divine metamorphosis [*cette divine et miraculeuse metamorphose*]."

The Ovidian provenance of this question for Montaigne will become clearer still as we examine what sort of a posture this "rising up" (*s'eslever*) really constitutes. Early in "An Apology for Raymond Sébond" Montaigne spoke of the difference between human and animal posture and of "that prerogative that the poets make much of, our erect stature [*stature droite*], looking toward heaven, its origin." Montaigne then cites Ovid, *Metamorphoses* 1:84–87:

While other animals face down to earth,
To man he gave a face raised to the skies
And to the stars he bade him lift his eyes. (trans. Frame, 336)

[*Pronáque cum spectent animalia catera terram,*
Os homini sublime dedit, caelúmque videre
Iussit, et erectos ad sidera tollere vultus]

Here Ovid is describing the moment of the emergence of the human, the moment of its being called or bidden to lift (*tollere*) its eyes skyward. Human being arises precisely "in the form [or effigy] of the all-controlling gods" (*in effigiem modernatum cuncta deorum*), or, in A. D. Melville's translation, "In likeness of the gods that govern the world"; "world" here in the sense of the total cycle or *cuncta*, which, as we have observed, is a key word that reappears in the poem's culminating cosmological vision in book 15, thus literally framing the entire work.

Montaigne, however, does not find Ovid's reasoning convincing, and he responds with an ironic edge that Shakespeare quickly made his own:

What animals do not have their face up high and in front, and do not look straight forward like ourselves, and do not discover, in their proper posture [*leur juste posture*], as much of heaven and earth as man? . . . Those that resemble us most are the ugliest and most abject of the whole band: for in external appearance [*apparence*] and shape of the face, it is the apes [*magots*]:

How similar the simian, ugliest of beasts!

[Ennius, cited by Cicero] (trans. Frame, 356; *Essais*, 2:170–71)

Montaigne's point is that there are, in fact, plenty of animals who share man's ability to look up or down. Furthermore, Montaigne is saying that the erstwhile sublime human paragon, who likes to believe he stands at the limits of transcendence, actually most resembles the *turpissima bestia,* the ugliest of beasts, the ape. The human will to transcendence is thus ironically brought down to size as an apish mimetic delusion. Ovid is thus like Montaigne's Seneca rather than his Plutarch. Like Montaigne, Shakespeare knew that we are never more susceptible to the apish "buzz" of transcendent pseudostatements than when we try to define the essence or the limits of the human. Like the painter of grotesque and fantastic shapes of whom Montaigne speaks at the beginning of "Of Friendship" (*De l'amitié*), what Montaigne himself produces (*Que sont-ce icy aussi?*) are but strange anamorphic texts composed of "grotesque and monstrous bodies, pieced together of divers members, without definite shape [*sans certaine figure*]" (trans. Frame, 135; *Essais* 1:198). Appearances shake where the figure slides toward the figureless.

What is important about Shakespeare's anamorphic, hendiadic articulation of the aporias of time is his consistent reinvention of a very subtle fetishism that refuses to choose between the time-fetish, between the "natural perspective" which is nature's own accidental anticipation of the most refined human artifice, and the unfigurable, nonphenomenal difference of the aporia itself. Beneath all his figurations for time, Shakespeare knows that there is only "the inaudible and noiseless foot of time" (*All's Well that Ends Well*, 5.3.41), whose hendiadic phrasing implies not simply that we cannot hear time, but that time does not in fact make a sound. "Like a fashionable host"

who takes the parting guest by the hand only in order to pull him back
into the party (*Troilus and Cressida* 3.3.159–62), Time effortlessly controls the world of becoming, and without any interest whatsoever in
dispensing justice:

> Time hath, my lord,
> A wallet at his back, wherein he puts
> Alms for oblivion, a great-sized monster
> Of ingratitudes. Those scraps are good deeds past,
> Which are devoured as fast as they are made.
> (*Troilus and Cressida* 3.3.139–44)

Time's relentless and monstrous consumption of the present leaves no
time for the remembrance of good deeds. Further still, this "great-
sized monster" is the world of becoming in its totality, and it is de-
vouring itself:

> Then everything includes itself in power,
> Power into will, will into appetite;
> And appetite, an universal wolf,
> So doubly seconded with will and power,
> Must perforce an universal prey,
> And last eat himself.
> (*Troilus and Cressida* 1.3.119–24)

When Graziano, for example, in *The Merchant of Venice* speaks deri-
sively of Shylock as a Pythagorean reincarnation of a bloodthirsty
wolf, or when in *Twelfth Night* the pagan Feste threatens the puritan
Malvolio that he will not release him from his squalid prison unless
he becomes a Pythagorean, the merely clownish surface of the humor
belies a profound fascination on Shakespeare's part with the vision of
the world in its entirety as a self-consuming and finite entity. If Feste
could persuade Malvolio to "fear to kill a woodcock lest thou dis-
possess the soul of thy grandam" (4.1.60), then perhaps a less preda-
tory world might begin to come into being, one that might slow the
inevitable auto-consumption of the world of power, will, and appetite. Shakespeare's anamorphic paragons are still part of his war with
Time, for they are his way of affirming, sometimes ironically, some-

times with tragic melancholy, that amid the unimaginable tedium of nature's endless cycles of creation and destruction there is "an art / Which does mend nature—change it rather—but / The art itself is nature" (*The Winter's Tale* 4.4.95–97). These accidental beauties that arise from "great creating nature" (89) were somehow enough to persuade Shakespeare that chance and fortune are worthy of determining our destiny.

III

The Moderns

The ideal of the most high-spirited, alive, and world-affirming
human being who has not only come to terms and learned to get
along with whatever was and is, but who wants to have *what
was and is* to all eternity, shouting insatiably *da capo* — not
only to a spectacle but at bottom to him who needs precisely this
spectacle — and who makes it necessary because again and again he
needs himself — and makes himself necessary — What? And this
wouldn't be — *circulus vitiosus deus?* NIETZSCHE,
Beyond Good and Evil § 56

I want to be a firebrand and a danger for all dry souls: glowing cinders
[*glühende Asche*] should fly before me. NIETZSCHE, *Nachlass*

5

Anamorphic Ghosts of Time:

Schopenhauer, Kant, and Hegel

Arthur Schopenhauer may have been (along with Marx and Freud) an exception among the major German philosophers inasmuch as his mastery of the English language and his deep familiarity with Shakespeare constituted a significant aspect of his philosophical activity. Although Nietzsche, like Kant, Hegel, and Heidegger, had no English, he had the good sense generally to emulate Schopenhauer's high regard for Shakespeare; and although he was more measured in his respect for Shakespeare's art, Nietzsche, as we will see later in this chapter, was far more daringly and revealingly speculative about Shakespeare than Schopenhauer could have imagined. I want to begin this chapter, however, by noting a strange, secret connection in Schopenhauer between Shakespeare and anamorphosis, so secret that Schopenhauer himself appears never to have noticed it, even though it touches on the central issues of his thinking.

The irony here is that while Schopenhauer adduced both Shakespeare and the Baroque optical techniques of anamorphosis at crucial moments in the articulation of his philosophy, he never suspected that this very connection was central to Shakespeare's own conception of his art. As we will see, this question bears centrally on Schopenhauer's idea of the will and his understanding of what is most essential in Kant's interpretation of the meaning of time. Schopenhauer conceived of his overall philosophical activity as defending Kant's thinking in its authentic form against its many detractors. And that is why Schopenhauer's comparison of the post-Kantian epoch in German philosophy

to the condition of English drama in Shakespeare's wake is the highest
honor he could possibly accord the poet:

Soon after Shakespeare's death, his dramas had to make way for those of
Ben Jonson, Massinger, Beaumont and Fletcher, and for a hundred years
had to yield supremacy to these. In the same way, Kant's serious philosophy was supplanted by Fichte's humbug, Schelling's eclecticism, and Jacobi's
mawkish and pious drivel, until in the end things went to such lengths that
an utterly wretched charlatan like Hegel was put on a level with, and even
rated much higher than, Kant. (Schopenhauer, "On Judgement, Criticism,
Approbation, and Fame," 456)

Schopenhauer's agon with Hegel underlies his general belligerence
vis-à-vis all the apparent heirs of Kant. Although Nietzsche knew
Schopenhauer's work much better than he ever grasped that of Hegel,
his contempt for Schopenhauer's spiritualizing ethos of denial and
world-weariness is not far removed from Hegel's determination to
think and imagine the form of the total system rather than the tedious
insistence of Kant and Schopenhauer (and later, as we will see, Heidegger himself) on the impossible incommensurability between human
history and what Kant called "the Ideals of pure reason." Like Hegel,
Nietzsche laughed at the residual religiosity of the Kantians, which
Schopenhauer took to its inevitable extreme with his morose advo-
cacy of a flight from becoming into an eternal, noumenal, hypostatic
nirvana. As remarked earlier, Nietzsche had, in *Philosophy in the Tragic
Age of the Greeks,* contrasted Schopenhauer's terror before the aporia
of time and the abyss of eternal return with Heraclitus's affirmation
of endless becoming. With this in mind, it is particularly curious that
Schopenhauer should adduce Shakespeare as a poetic stand-in for the
great Kant himself. But Schopenhauer himself has no misgivings or
doubts about his sense that Shakespeare understood the workings of
fate. He regarded Shakespeare as "one of the ancients" and liked to cite
the phrase, "Fate show thy force" (*Twelfth Night* 1.5.314). Like Nietzsche and Hegel, we will soon recognize that Schopenhauer in fact does
everything to ensure that the sensible forms of fate, time, and the Will
will never show themselves, other than, that is, in the abstract spiritual

medium of a realm of pure ideality utterly removed, in some unimaginable fashion, from all traces of the world of becoming.

What Schopenhauer regarded as his Shakespearean-Kantian effort to grasp "the unity of the deep-lying root of necessity and contingency" ("Transcendent Speculation on the Apparent Deliberateness in the Fate of the Individual," 210) is really an effort to understand the will in itself as something immaterial, a kind of nothingness, that moves through time and the world of becoming toward the nothingness and the extinction proper to it. What Schopenhauer's notion of fate shows is that there is nothing to show, that everything is in fact an illusory veil. And this is the point where anamorphosis becomes important for Schopenhauer, because it enacts optically, within the visual field, the larger and more properly Schopenhauerian movement from phenomenality to the stasis of disembodied, de-realized substance. While Hegel sought to redefine the noumenal as a hitherto unsuspected dimension of difference, absence, and negativity within phenomenality itself, Schopenhauer took exactly the opposite course and widened the fissure between phenomena and noumena and yet at the same time insisted on being able to characterize the thing-in-itself in ways that would have no doubt horrified Kant. Remember that for Schopenhauer "matter is the *will* itself, yet no longer in itself, but in so far as it is perceived." Matter is thus "the visibility of the will in general" (*The World as Will and Representation*, 2:308–9). Moreover, since Schopenhauer believes in the "will's turning away from life as the ultimate aim of temporal existence" ("Transcendent Speculation," 223), it becomes clear that anamorphic perspectives provided Schopenhauer with an excellent analogy within the visual field for the movement of fate through the world of representation as the motion of a noumenal will through the world of becoming and back to itself. The question of whether this return constitutes a circle in Schopenhauer is just the question Schopenhauer wishes most to avoid, for his goal is to imagine the final extinction of the cycles. And this may also explain why Schopenhauer should adduce the one anamorphic technique that Shakespeare never mentions, which is the use of the conical mirror. There the confusion of the painted image is most extreme, and the resolution of the image on the conical mirror, which is placed at roughly the center point of the painting, is vividly differentiated from the blurred shapes on the surface beneath.

In his essay "Transcendent Speculation on the Apparent Deliber-ateness in the Fate of the Individual," Schopenhauer sets the stage for conical anamorphosis when he describes "the path" of fate that rules over the course of a life in an effort to differentiate and empha-size the really blind chance that his notion of fate constitutes, "which is absolutely nothing in itself and which dispenses with all direction and order":

> Just as there are certain images or figures called anamorphoses which re-veal to the naked eye only distorted, mutilated, and shapeless objects, but, on the other hand, show as regular human figures when seen in a conical mirror, so the purely empirical apprehension of the course of the world is like that intuitive perception of the picture with the naked eye; the pursuit of fate's purpose, on the other hand, is like the intuitive perception in the conical mirror which combines and arranges what has there been scattered apart. ("Transcendent Speculation," 206)

It is important to say that nothing could show more clearly how far Schopenhauerian anamorphosis differs from Shakespeare's in the relatively simple way it constructs its time-fetish, here "fate's purpose," which he defines a few pages later: "What presents and maintains the phenomenal world is the *will* that also lives and strives in every indi-vidual" (218). Shakespeare's fetish is doubly bound and more com-plexly combined and arranged. Even so, it is to Shakespeare himself, and more particularly *Macbeth,* that Schopenhauer turns when he wants to express the tragic structure of human experience, which is "forcibly driven [by the will] to turn away from life and to arrive at regeneration by a Caesarian operation so to speak" (233). I believe Schopenhauer means to say that the will lives its strange life-in-death only by virtue of its capacity to give birth to itself through a kind of Caesarian birth and untimely ripping from the womb, which is to say that the will rips itself out of becoming, out of time, and sub-lates itself into eternity. Schopenhauer concludes his essay by focusing on "the hour of death" as a focal point for the "mysterious forces" of our "eternal fate," which "crowd together and come into action" in a characteristically lurid moment of the Schopenhauerian occult. Schopenhauer's ascetic-Buddhist-Christian leap marks the terrain of Nietzschean eternal recurrence with the force of its effort to escape time and becoming.

There is no disputing the fact that Kant brought to an end whole regimes of phrases and discourses about the meaning of time and made it impossible once and for all for one to believe that speaking about true time or about the absolute cosmos was of any value at all. But by the same token, Kant's antinomical diffidence about the question of time (e.g., "the relations of time lie entirely outside the concepts of understanding" [*Critique of Pure Reason*, 169/B159]) made the difference between the aporia of time and the time-fetish more comprehensible than ever before. To forbid oneself to speak about absolute time or space is to feel, as Kant says openly in § 27 of *The Critique of Judgement*, that the ideas of reason are of greater value than invented images of the total system. Kant's celebration of the powerlessness of the imagination as having greater value than an image of the absolute cosmos reinforces the most familiar sacrificial scenarios. After Nietzsche, it is difficult to be patient with the idealizing narcissism and the calculating piety of the so-called iconoclast. One might even say, at the risk of slight exaggeration, that Nietzschean eternal recurrence is really only the realization of the fundamentally antinomical character of the religious and ideological notions that Kant called "the Ideals of pure reason." As Hegel and Schelling realized, although a certain imagelessness still defines the position of our modernity, things might not always be so; and so, very unlike Schopenhauer, both Hegel and Schelling have no difficulty thinking about eternal return in ways that are both familiar and inventive.

But let us finish with Schopenhauer, and with what his sort of extreme idealization of Kant might tell us about the secret history of eternal recurrence. Although not a subtle metafetishist, Schopenhauer's construction of his Kantian time-fetish is not without interest: "Kant's proposition that the thing-in-itself is unknowable is therefore modified by me to the extent of saying that it is not *absolutely* and entirely knowable, but that the clearest and most immediate of its phenomena, differing from all the others through the directness of its being known, acts for us as its substitute" (*Manuscript Remains,* 3:40–41). Schopenhauer's collation of a certain identity between mind and will acts as this substitute, and effectively reduces Schopenhauer's doctrine of the will to a baldly occult fiction. The fetish of a collective mental substance that exists in another temporality, one where duration has been suspended, is what Schopenhauer relies on in his "Essay on Spirit Seeing" and other well-known essays on dreams and clairvoyance: "In some dreams, clairvoyant somnambulism, and second sight, that deceptive form [of time in which the future does not seem to exist at all] is temporarily pushed aside and the future then manifests itself as the present" ("Ideas Concerning the Intellect," 43). Schopenhauer's odd notion that "clairvoyants can think with other people's brains" ("Essay on Spirit Seeing," 305) would appear as a sort of Kantian symptom, or at least the expression of the extremity to which one Kantian disciple went in order to ensure that the noumenal realm itself was free of the antinomical flux of becoming. Although Kant's texts reopen all the pathways that had been closed by metaphysics, it cannot be denied that Kant bristled at the thought of a cosmos or an ontology in which the thing-in-itself was at odds with itself: "the real in things cannot be in conflict with itself" (*Critique of Pure Reason,* 288/A280/B336). The *Ding-an-sich* is thus already quarantined or sequestered from time. The very "scope of the time-concept [*Zeitinbegriff*]" (*Critique of Pure Reason,* 184/A145/B185) is thus determined in advance, and it is done so precisely in order to mark off the noumenal realm from the antinomies of time. Although the direction that Hegel and Schelling would take is also marked in Kant's texts, it should be clear that Schopenhauer was enacting some deepseated presuppositions about time and Being in Kant's thinking. In a fundamental way, and regardless of whether it goes against the grain of what we want to think about Kant's antinomy of time, Schopenhauer really did succeed in thinking Kant's "thought out to the end" (Schopenhauer, "Fragments for a History of Philosophy," 132).

And so it is not surprising that Schopenhauer, as a good Kantian, should prove so adept at circumventing time. A passage from one of his last essays gives a sense of his final position on time and recurrence:

How could nature throughout endless time endure the maintenance of forms and the renewal of individuals, the countless repetition of the life-process, without becoming weary, unless her own innermost kernel were something timeless and thus wholly indestructible, a thing-in-itself quite different from its phenomena, something metaphysical that is distinct from everything physical? This is the *will* in ourselves and in everything. ("Some Observations on the Antithesis of the Thing-in-Itself and the Phenomenon," 95).

Schopenhauer was a tremendously convenient object-lesson for Nietzsche that clearly indicated the fetish character of the will in German idealism. And so time is relegated to the realm of appearance, while will takes the role of essence. Time is a mere empty form of subjectivity that is, as Schopenhauer says, filled with the "essential nature" of the will. The merely "formal qualities" of time are kept, in good Kantian fashion, from intruding upon "the essential nature [that] fills the whole of time" (*Manuscript Remains*, 4:707). We have already seen this problem in what I called Shakespeare's "war with Time," where the supposed essence that appears in time is at once of time itself and yet somehow distinct and separable. Schopenhauer fought tirelessly in this war. He always struggled against thinking the identity of time and the will, since although "the will makes itself known in successive acts" (*Manuscript Remains*, 3:353), that is, in time, it is not of time: "No death disturbs the will which, as thing-in-itself, lies outside time" (*Manuscript Remains*, 3:544).

Those non-Kantians among us who can think only "through the optical lens of time" do not have a clairvoyantlike access to the *Ding-an-sich* and to "that mechanism which is hidden in the background, and from which everything originates: and that is the thing-in-itself as *primum mobile* the mechanism that imparts to the whole complicated and variegated plaything of this world" ("Essay on Spirit Seeing," 264). Schopenhauer sometimes appears to toy with the idea that perhaps time were somehow decisive to the motion of the will, citing Schelling's idea that "gravity is the entire and indivisible God" and F. Max Müller's notes to the *Rig Veda:* "Brahma means originally *force, will,* wish, and the propulsive power of creation" (*Manuscript*

Remains, 4:189; 376–77); but the idea that time might be the transcendental concept for the reality of the universal motion of the absolute cosmos never really reached him. We might say that Nietzsche's thought emerged as the counterforce to Schopenhauer's formidable resistance to eternal return. But Schopenhauer seems so close at times to breaking through:

> The *ideality of time,* discovered by Kant, is really contained already in the *law of inertia* appertaining to mechanics. For at bottom, this law states that mere *time* is incapable of producing any physical effect; thus by itself and alone, time effects no change in the rest or motion of a body. We see from this that time is not something physically real, but transcendentally ideal, in other words, that it has its origins not in things, but in the knowing subject. ("Ideas Concerning the Intellect," 38–39)

Safely shut off in the ghettolike enclosure of inner sense and the formation of mental representations, time can never be more than the ineffective form of subjective ideation which "passes over things without making the slightest impression thereon." Nothing could be more remote from "essence-in-itself [which] exists in the *Nunc stans,*" the "eternal now" in which, as instances of the will, "we ourselves stand" (47–48).

Schopenhauer was horrified by the "monstrous perversity" of what he insisted on regarding as the primacy of the concept in Hegel ("Essay on Spirit Seeing," 294). I suspect that Schopenhauer never comprehended Hegel's notion of the belonging-together of concept and essence as constituting in fact the most rigorously Kantian dimension of his thinking, which is to say that the insistence on the concept takes seriously Kant's sense of the subjective limitations that demand the strictures of transcendental thought, whose virtue is exactly that it recognizes individual being, this chiasmus of particularizing perception and universalizing reflection, as that which alone has being. Without first negotiating the materiality of subjectivization, which includes the form of its language and its concepts, no other modality of Being could possibly be accessible. With Heidegger, Hegel would agree that Kant steers everything toward the transcendental reflection of an individual subject. In other words, Hegel regards spirit's notion of belonging to eternity as being precisely the way it experiences time. While Kant wants to insist that, with respect to the absolute cosmos, he "holds out no prospect of a limit" (*Critique of Judgement* § 27), Hegel wants to imagine precisely such a limit, and to assert the idea of infinite time as a circle: "The image of true infinity [*wahrhafte Unendlichkeit*], bent back into itself [*in sich zurückgebogen*], becomes the *circle,* the line which has reached itself, which is closed and wholly present, without *beginning* and *end*" (Hegel, *Science of Logic,* 149; *Werke* 5:164). Hegel's circle of "true infinity" anticipates the central issues of Nietzsche's doctrine. Affirmative annihilation and annihilating affirmation describe the contradictory, antinomical work of time in Hegel's thinking. The infinite for Hegel is "the consummated return into self [*in sich Zurückgekehrtsein*]," the endless negativity of an eternally impossible return that keeps returning eternally, endlessly "turning back on itself."

Spirit's antinomical experience of time marks both the aporetic limit of Kantian transcendental reflection and the beginning of Hegel's speculative invention. In this remarkable passage from his *Lectures on the History of Philosophy,* Hegel unveils a Kant who "shows here too much tenderness for things," which is to say too much concern to allow the mere idea of contradiction to get too close to anything that might look like essence:

Transcendental idealism lets the contradiction remain, only if it is not Being in itself that is thus contradictory, for the contradiction has its source in our thought alone. Thus the same antinomy remains in our mind [*Gemüte*] and as it was formerly God who had to take upon Himself all contradictions, so now it is self-consciousness. But the Kantian philosophy does not go on to grapple with the fact that it is not things that are contradictory, but self-consciousness itself. Experience teaches that the ego does not melt away by reason of these contradictions, but continues to exist; we need not therefore trouble ourselves about its contradictions, for it can bear them [*ertragen*]. Nevertheless Kant shows here too much tenderness for things [*zuviel Zärtlichkeit für die Dinge*]. But that spirit [*Geist*], which is far higher, should be a contradiction—that is not a pity at all [*kein Schade*]. The contradiction is therefore by no means solved by Kant. The world of appearances has an aspect that he does not reach [*dem kommt er nicht zu*]. This is an other as spirit [*Dieses ist ein Anderes als der Geist*]. Contradiction destroys itself; and that is why spirit in itself is all derangement and disorder [*Zerrüttung, Verrücktheit*]. The true solution would be found in the statement that the categories have no truth in themselves, and the Unconditioned of Reason [*das Unbedingte der Vernunft*] just as little, but that it lies in the unity of both as concrete, and in that alone. (*Lectures on the History of Philosophy*, 3:451 [trans. modified]; *Werke*, 20:359)

Hegel's argument is really a hyperbolic irony, for he in effect maintains that Kant is not sufficiently Kantian, which is why Kant missed that "aspect" (*Ansich*) of the "world of appearances" (*Erscheinungswelt*) that is the utter disorder of spirit. What this means above all is that Hegel clearly recognized Kant's altogether unnecessary timidity in pretending to protect *die Dinge* from the ravages of time and its antinomies. More precisely, Hegel points to the Christian scene of sacrifice in Kant, where the quiet martyrdom of self-consciousness stands in lieu of Christ's crucifixion. Spirit is the concrete "unity" (*Einheit*), and Hegel has none of Kant's pity for its difficulties and divisions but chooses instead to affirm the negative work of the spirit. In this respect, Schopenhauer was even more tenderhearted than Kant, and went to even greater lengths to avoid having to face the out-of-joint character of the time of internal consciousness and the time of perception. Hegel is very ironic toward Kant when he pretends to assure him that the ego can bear the burden of irresolvable contradictions. While Schopenhauer turned to the crude fetish of an eternal will, Hegel constructs the subtle fetish of dialectical double negation.

Everything we have had to say thus far about the double articulation of the aporia and the fetish of time is fully anticipated by Hegel, in, among other places, the closing pages of the *Phenomenology of Spirit*, where time "appears as the destiny and necessity of spirit that is not complete in (it)self" (487). Even though it may not yet be present, the "unity" between the concept of the existent and its actual Being (*Sein*) is what Hegel calls the "Idea" (*Idee*), toward which spirit's work of negation relentlessly strives. And while Kant foreclosed in advance the very possibility that such striving might be purposeful, Hegel's thought is oriented toward this Idea as the culminating *eidos* or concept that could calculate the time of the absolute cosmos. We might say that Nietzsche's doctrine of return is really a kind of Hegelian "speculative unity" (*spekulativer Einheit*) with respect to time and spirit.

In *Glas* Derrida cites a central passage in Hegel's account of time and spirit in the *Phenomenology of Spirit* and comments on it immediately afterwards in brackets:

> *Time* is the *concept* itself that *is there* (*der* da ist) and which represents itself (*sich vorstellt*) to consciousness as empty intuition; for this reason, spirit necessarily appears (*erscheint*) in time, and it appears in time just so long (*so lange* [!]) as it has not *grasped* its pure concept, i.e. has not annulled (*tilgt*) time [*tilgen:* destroy, annihilate, efface, abolish, annul, for example a debt; *eine Schuld tilgen;* to annul, cancel, or pay off a debt, a mistake; *eine Rente tilgen:* to redeem an annuity]. (Derrida, *Glas,* 228, citing Hegel, *Phenomenology,* 487)

These are Derrida's parentheses and brackets, and his point is clearly that Hegel's spirit mistakes its own orientation to time, which is why Derrida inserts the exclamation mark after *so lange,* as if spirit had any choice in the matter. Derrida's irony vis-à-vis spirit's relation to time is precisely what is missing in Hegel. Were Hegel more ironic he would have less difficulty affirming the temporal horizon of the will and essence of spirit.

Hegel began the reinvention of the Kantian critical revolution as the effort to take the measure of the ontico-ontological difference, even though his own habits of thought could barely sustain the ironic edge necessary to pare beings away from their delusory appropriation of the meaning of Being. Nietzsche and Heidegger have been the great beneficiaries of Hegel's thought of difference as a *real relation* to Being. They, of course, step beyond Hegel's still onto-theological position and reflect whether Being might be permanently in default, missing. The ultimate irony we face in the modern epoch is the possibility that, as Heidegger puts it, "Being as difference [. . .] may well remain wholly without an object" (Heidegger, *Identity and Difference,* 64).

Once Kant opened the path to thinking presence as difference, all bets were off, and philosophy could no longer anticipate that there might henceforth be any moment of stabilizing reappropriation whereby beings could rediscover a path that would lead them, through the difference, and back to Being once again, which Hegel's spirit still imagines possible. Zarathustra rails at his animals when they build poetic bridges back to Being because he knows perfectly well that they are only childish simulacra. But that is exactly Nietzsche's point: that we always build impossible and artificial pathways that lead nowhere and only in order to bury the monstrous reality of difference, and that that is what the will to power is all about.

To conclude with Hegel, let us take the example of the first moment of the history of natural religion and of the subject's relation to Being as a relation to the blinding light of the sun. This is the first moment of spirit's relation to time, and it is one of a seemingly absolute aporia. Hegel writes at the end of the *Phenomenology of Spirit* of "effusions of light [*Lichtgüsse*]; in their simplicity, they are at the same time [*zugleich*] its [spirit's] becoming-for-(it)self and the return from its being-there [*sein Fürsichwerden und Rückkehr aus seinem Dasein*], torrents of fire destructive of figuration [*die Gestaltung verzehrende Feuerströme*]" (419–20). All the tension of modernity vis-à-vis time is evident in this passage; for on the one hand, this fire destroys all form, and yet on the other hand, and *at the same time,* as though there were some underlying sameness, some shared *substance,* Hegel speaks of this moment as the *return* of spirit to itself, to its proper Dasein; its being-there as spirit is thus also its belonging-with or to these streams of fire. Here is Derrida's commentary: "This first figure of natural religion figures the absence of figure, a purely visible, thus invisible sun that allows seeing without showing itself or that shows itself without showing anything, consuming all in its phenomenon: *die Gestalt der Gestaltlosigkeit*" (*Glas,* 238). "The form of formlessness," or "the figure of figurelessness," is Hegel's very subtle fetish for spirit's (non-) relation to time, for the antinomical possibility of both at once. Although the dialectical resolution of this antinomy may at some point be possible, there remains for us still only the difference between the aporia of time and the fetish-idea of spirit's imaginary return to itself.

6

Drive-Time: Eternal Return and the Life of the

Instincts in Schelling, Freud, and the Marquis de Sade

If Nietzsche's doctrine of eternal recurrence illuminated the place of the discourses on time vis-à-vis the forms of value, permanence, and power it did so only by working through Kant, Schopenhauer, and Hegel and by engaging the antinomical character of Being and becoming in a more complex manner. One might even say, by way of a certain historical accident, Nietzsche remains most rigorously Kantian in the very attempt to posit a condition of possibility as an actuality and a necessity. Nietzsche takes perhaps more seriously than anyone the subjectivization of positing in Kant and Fichte when he insists on the self-overcoming his doctrine entails, which means that I become myself only at the moment of an absolute self-annihilation, that I am most myself when I conceive of myself as the necessary accident of an immense sea of differences.

Of course Heidegger is correct when he protests that Nietzsche's doctrine is simply the last and consummate statement of modern metaphysics with its assumption of an underlying rational substance linking beings and Being. What Heidegger misses in Nietzsche's doctrine is precisely its way of snatching victory from the jaws of defeat by reinventing the absolute indifference of Being to beings in the form of the eternal recurrence of the individual being in its self-identical sameness. At the very moment beings are utterly lost to Being *in fact*, Nietzsche proposes that, in time, in some still distant future, human beings will reaffirm themselves against all the opposing forces of chance and necessity and re-ontologize the presence of their difference against the horizon of an eternal sameness. What makes this rhetorical and ideological inflection so important to Nietzsche is his sense that the instinctual demands of humans to live and to empower themselves within the world will at some point bring them to his doctrine as an effort to reverse the instinctual depletion of long centuries of nihilism. In the meantime we remain in the regime of difference, where *Anwesenheit* or presence is determined by difference and not yet by the Being of the eternal return of the same. Nietzschean eternal return continues Hegel's thinking of presence as somehow eternally sustained by difference: the eternal return of the same play of difference.

In his *Lectures on the History of Philosophy* Hegel characterized Friedrich Schelling's thinking as a kind of essentialization of difference, which means that he believed Schelling thought of the difference between the relative position of spirit vis-à-vis the general system as an "essential relation": "There is only essential relation, relative identity; the difference therein present thus ever remains [*Es ist nur wesentliche Beziehung, relative Identität; der Unterschied bleibt immer darin*]" (3:522–23; *Werke* 20:431). This fully anticipates Nietzsche's perspectivism. Schelling's sense of a resistant difference that cannot be dialectically reappropriated, à la Hegel, by the historical phenomenology of spirit, perhaps presents a keener challenge to Hegelian dialectics than even Nietzsche. For Schelling human history is the flight from the terror of the difference toward the more comfortable periphery of the self-same. This is from his "Philosophical Inquiry into the Essence of Human Freedom" (1809): "The terror of life drives man out of the center in which he was created; for being the lucid and pure essence of all will this is consuming fire for each particular will; in order to be able to live in it man must mortify all egotism, which almost makes necessary the attempt to leave it and to enter the periphery in order to seek peace for his selfhood there" (*Of Human Freedom*, 59). We might say that the history of philosophy has been a long flight from the mortifying fires of difference.

Nietzsche seems to have been unaware of Schelling's ideas, even though, as Karl Löwith has remarked, "Schelling is the sole thinker of German idealism who—in spite of his theogonic constructions— has a positive relationship to Nietzsche's teaching of the eternal cycle"

(*Nietzsche's Philosophy of the Eternal Recurrence of the Same*, 146).
What seems to me most distinctive about Schelling is his way of drawing analogies between the individual subject's dilemma in time and
the emergence of time itself, of that first "consuming fire" through
which both time and human Dasein must pass. Drawing on the 1809
treatise *Of Human Freedom* and the important drafts of *The Ages of
the World* (*Die Weltalter*), which Schelling wrote during the following
year, Slavoj Žižek provides a clear and timely defense of Schelling's
vision of ontological difference and grasps how Schelling eludes both
the traditional Platonist hierarchy of eternity over time and becoming
(which he does by insisting that eternity is an inchoate and lesser,
not greater, modality of existence than time) and the Heideggerian
notion that temporality is the ultimate horizon of Being: "nowhere is
Schelling farther from Heidegger, from his analytics of finitude, than
in his conception of the relationship between time and eternity. For
Schelling, eternity is not a modality of time; it is rather time itself
that is a specific mode (or rather modification) of eternity: Schelling's
supreme effort is to *'deduce' time itself from the deadlock of eternity*"
(*The Abyss of Freedom*, 29). It is the struggle of the eternal will with
itself that enables time to disengage itself from eternity: "Since eternity is unconsciously impelled to seek itself, a self-sufficient will *produces* itself in eternity. *Eternity is not conscious of this will*, [whose production occurs] independently of it, and in a manner unintelligible
to it" (Schelling, *Ages of the World*, trans. Norman, 137). In Schelling's
system the will that surges forth into time and becoming is the very
foundation of an eternally recurrent temporality, or rather, to use
Schelling's idiom, the eternal *reproduction* of the time-will in eternity.

There are many analogies and contrasts to be made between Schelling's work of 1809/10 and Nietzsche's doctrine of return, and perhaps even more connections between Nietzsche and Heidegger to
Schelling's later, so-called "positive philosophy" where reason points
"ek-statically" to those modalities, or "potencies," of existence that lie
beyond reason itself (cf. Fackenheim, "Schelling's Philosophy of Religion"). In his new mythology of reason, Schelling conceived of "the
ever-renewing movement of eternity" (*Ages of the World*, trans. Bolman, 116) as an immense rotary drive mechanism that worked to re-

turn eternity and the eternal will of temporality to their primordial deadlock. Schelling's vision of three rotary drive-cycles that ceaselessly reconfigure time and eternity from past to present, present to future, and future to past seems to me to anticipate Freud's theory of the drive mechanisms, *Eros* and *Thanatos*, as much as it does the Nietzschean *Kreislauf.*

It is to Schelling that Freud says he owes his understanding of "the 'uncanny'": "We notice that Schelling says something which throws quite a new light on the concept of the *Unheimlich,* for which we were certainly not prepared. According to him, everything is *unheimlich* that ought to have remained secret and hidden but has come to light" ("The 'Uncanny,'" *SE* 17:225). Freudian psychoanalysis is in several respects heir to Schelling's philosophy of nature. The doctrine of return is the hidden secret in the history of philosophy that seems to be endlessly re- and de-sublimated from one historical epoch to the next.

I want to consider two moments in Freud's writing that link the eternal recurrence of the same to the life of the instinctual drive mechanisms and to the speculation regarding the emergence of organic life. These issues are as much Nietzsche's as they are Schelling's, and it is above all the "uncanniness" of the question of an eternal or infinite cycle of temporal events or great years in Freud's thinking that I want to emphasize more than his specific philological debt to a text or a thinker. In fact, let us begin at the end of Freud's career where he speculated on a possible identity, even the recurrence of the same, between Empedocles's "cosmic phantasy" and his own practice of psychoanalysis. Empedocles is the name that comes to Freud's mind in this passage from "Analysis Terminable and Interminable" (1937), in which he inscribes the history of psychoanalysis as a chapter in the secret history of eternal recurrence:

> But the theory of Empedocles which especially deserves our interest is one which approximates so closely to the psychoanalytic theory of the instincts that we should be tempted to maintain that the two are identical, if it were not for the difference that the Greek philosopher's theory is a cosmic phantasy [*kosmische Phantasie*] while ours is content to claim biological validity. . . .

. . . Empedocles thought of the process of the universe [*Weltprozess*] as a continuous, never-ceasing alternation of periods [*fortgesetzte, niemals auf-hörende Abwechslung von Perioden*], in which the one or the other of the two fundamental forces gains the upper hand, so that at one time love [*philia*] and at another strife [*neikos*] puts its purpose completely into effect and dominates the universe, after which the other, vanquished side asserts itself and in its turn defeats its partner. . . .

. . . And no one can foresee in what guise the nucleus of truth [*Wahr-heitskern*] contained in the theory of Empedocles will present itself to later understanding. (*SE* 23:245–47)

Presumably, then, German philosophy and psychoanalysis are "guises" for the eternal recurrence of the doctrine of return. In its final phase Freud's theory of the instincts "sought to solve the riddle of life by supposing that these two instincts [*Eros/Thanatos*] were struggling with each other from the very first" (*Beyond the Pleasure Principle, SE* 18:61). From the Pythagoreans, Plato, Plotinus, and Schelling, there is a direct progression to Freud's notion that the realm of the sexual, or life, instincts is, at its inception, bound up with "the death instincts" which display "*a need to restore an earlier state of things*" (*SE* 18:57). Between them, this instinctual struggle between love and strife opens a temporal singularity and pulls it toward its close. It is not so important, Freud remarks in a footnote, that "the doctrine of transmigration" in Plato should have Oriental or Pythagorean sources; what matters is that "it had struck him as containing an element of truth" (*Beyond the Pleasure Principle* 18:58n.).

I want to look a little more closely at an essay from 1907 called "Delusions and Dreams in Jensen's *Gradiva*" because there Freud focuses again and again on Jensen's insistent language of return and recurrence, whose plainly Nietzschean resonance he never, however, mentions, even though Freud is adducing Jensen's story as a veritable paradigm of his own theory of psychoanalysis. If the passage we cited above from "Analysis Terminable and Interminable" pointed to the esoteric secret affinity between psychoanalysis and the doctrine of re-turn, then Freud's analysis of Jensen's novel, which is an early work best known for containing Freud's first account of the therapeutic

goals of analysis, should be regarded as Freud's early effort at encrypt-
ing eternal return as the secret "kernel" of psychoanalytic truth.

Like Empedocles, Jensen presents in another "guise" a lesson exactly
identical to that of psychoanalysis: "The procedure which the author
makes his Zoë adopt for curing her childhood friend's delusion shows
a far-reaching similarity — no, a complete agreement in its essence —
with a therapeutic method which was introduced into medical practice in 1895 by Dr. Josef Breuer and myself, and to the perfecting of
which I have since then devoted myself" (*SE* 9:88–89). The sameness and identity between the two projects are particularly striking
since everything, every detail, virtually every word, in *Gradiva* and in
Freud's essay, relates somehow to the themes of return and repetition.
Stranger still, I want to demonstrate that Freud's reading seems blind
not only to Jensen's rhetoric of recurrence but also, and perhaps much
more damagingly, to Freud's credibility as an analyst, to the issues
of gay panic and fetishism, which I will argue are central to Jensen's
vision of his protagonist's illness and delusions.

Norbert Hanold's childhood friend, Zoë Bertgang, takes the part of
analyst and lover in order to cure her childhood friend of his hallucinations of the ghostly Gradiva by making him realize that she herself
is Gradiva and that his visions of her as an ancient Pompeiian were
the result of his long-repressed affection for her. Central to the novel
is Norbert's unconscious translation of the German *Bertgang* into the
Latin *Gradiva,* both of which mean "stride" or "gait," and thus relate the name to the centerpiece of Norbert's phantasies: his obsession
with the fetishlike position of a woman's foot, suspended, frozen, as
it were, in the midst of her stride with one foot pointing downward.
Freud only mentions and does not emphasize at all the fetish character
of Norbert's delusions, nor does he appear to note that the symptom
lingers even after Norbert's apparent "cure." Since his emphasis is on
the efficacy of analysis, perhaps he either didn't see or pretended not
to see Norbert's apparent resistance to therapy.

At the very end of Jensen's novel, after Norbert has been apparently
cured of his visions of Gradiva and of his disgust at all expressions
of heterosexual desire (save, of course, those expressions that involve
the woman's perpendicular foot), his analyst-lover, Zoë, who seems to

understand Norbert much better than Freud, raises her dress slightly
in order to give Norbert a glimpse of that curiously inflected foot,
which she knows is still the focal point of his desire: "Gradiva *rediviva*
Zoë Bertgang, viewed by him with dreamily observing eyes" (Jensen,
Gradiva, 235). Zoë knows that Norbert is a very subtle fetishist who
has learned how to affirm and to deny castration. I have a problem,
not only with Freud's oddly obtuse reading of Jensen with regard to
Zoë/Gradiva's foot (which is the crucial element in the "rebirth" of
Gradiva as Zoë), but with his overall evasion of the issue of Norbert's
sexual orientation. Freud wants only to maintain that Zoë, as a stand-
in for psychoanalysts everywhere, has succeeded in leading her lover
into an apparently normal heterosexual relationship. Freud did not
think it was necessary to ask whether *Gradiva* might also be a kind of
"how to" book about a homoerotic fetishist's successful masquerade
as a heterosexual. And yet Jensen sends some very clear signals, not
only with the closing glimpse of the phallic foot, but with a wistful eye
to the future when he writes that Zoë's heart clings to Norbert "perhaps so unwisely" (Jensen, *Gradiva*, 233).

Still more important, although somewhat less obvious, is the setting Jensen chooses for Norbert's most delusional visions: the house
of Meleager. Norbert remarks to Gradiva at the height of his illness:
"On that account the Greek poet, Meleager, came to my mind and I
thought that you were one of his descendants and were returning —
in the hour which you are allowed — to your ancestral home" (*Gradiva*, 197). The noontide ghosts of this ancient house may be calling
to Norbert in a quite fundamental sense. Just what this ancestry constitutes might be clearer if we recall that Meleager (140–70 B.C.) was
the poet of homoerotic epigrams: "I was thirsty. / It was hot. / I kissed
the boy / with girl-soft skin. / My thirst was quenched" (*Poems of Meleager*, #17). We must, it seems, displace Freud's emphasis in at least
two places: first, the prosthetic phallic function of the fetish foot is
really Norbert's great achievement; and second, we should conceive
of it *not* as something he should have to overcome or surmount but as
something that enables him to negotiate his desire for Zoë, even if, as
Jensen seems to suspect, his heterosexual masquerade is just that and
thus may not last very long.

"Delusion and Dream" is from 1907, at a point in Freud's thinking when he was not ready to admit the force or complexity of the dynamic of repetition in which the symptom was articulated. It seems to me plausible to assume that what Freud found most unreadable in Jensen was the Nietzschean resonance of his language. What Freud resists in reading *Gradiva* may be as important as what he thinks he's reading. Jensen's novel is about the return of the ghosts of the ancient world, about hallucinations in broad daylight (e.g., "only at the midday hour"), about the wavering of a male German intellectual's sexual orientation, and about the shrewd effort of a young woman to lure his desire in her direction by affecting a very singular way of walking. One might even suspect that Norbert's Zarathustra-like midday frenzy amid the return of ancient ghosts is more than just a vague recollection of Nietzsche. If Norbert is a kind of Nietzsche, then perhaps Nietzsche is also a kind of Norbert, whose ambivalent sexual orientation may be linked to his experience of the return of something ancient.

The return of a ghost from the cataclysm that destroyed Pompeii almost two millennia ago is Jensen's version of eternal return. Although it is more properly a kind of *anacyclosis* or a Viconian *ricorso* than a Pythagorean *metakosmesis,* Gradiva's return reveals a pattern of historical recurrence that relates to a more profound substratum of sameness within nature itself. The singularity and difference marked out in Gradiva's recurrent form must look, of course, to the foot as its signature moment. And that is why it is so important that Jensen should emphasize the fact that the bas-relief of Gradiva is precisely identical to that of Zoë down to every detail, including the foot. For Jensen, if not for Freud, what returns is not only the structural opposition of desire and conscience but the reemergence of an exact physical sameness, including the relatively bizarre anomaly of the erect foot.

Freud is also, however, alert to the question of time, though only in the context of the "struggle" between what (at this early point in his thinking) he called the "sexual instincts" and "ego instincts," a "struggle" which "is in fact unending [*geht eigentlich nie zu ende*]" (*SE* 9:52). He reiterates this point with a citation from Horace (*Epistles* I, 10.24): "You may drive out Nature with a pitchfork, but she will always

return [*Naturam expelles furca, tamen usque recurret*]" (*SE* 9:35). Here
Freud comes closest to the spirit of Jensen's novel. And like Jensen,
Freud repeatedly uses the word *Wiederkehr* (e.g., Freud, *Die Wahn
und die Träume in W. Jensens 'Gradiva,' Gesammelte Werke* 7:47, 58–59,
60–61, 99, et al.). Freud is most concerned of course with the temporality of return within the experience of an individual who suddenly
falls ill and develops symptoms, in other words, with what enables the
initial repression to become dislodged from the unconscious and to
begin to emerge into consciousness: "It is precisely what was chosen
as the instrument of repression—like the *'furca'* [pitchfork] of the
Latin saying—that becomes the carrier of the thing recurring [*der Trä-
ger des Wiederkehrenden*]: in and behind the repressing force, what is
repressed proves itself victor in the end. . . . The repressed in its recurrence [*bei seiner Wiederkehr*] emerges from the repressing force itself"
(*SE* 9:35, trans. modified). What Norbert has repressed is his confusion about the castration of women, which is disturbed by the ancient
bas-relief of Gradiva. What Freud is pointing out here is the uncanny
power of the recurrent symptom to take the form of the very thing that
brought on the repression in the first place: the representation of the
repressing agent becomes the representation of the reemerging symptom; the very thing that buried the memory becomes the very thing
that brings it back after a long period of latency. Foot fetishism is of
course a metonymy for a prosthetic body part whose mere proximity
to the genitals makes it a likely object with which to cover an unac-
ceptable absence. Freud, however, does not take the argument in this
direction but turns instead to an etching by Felicien Rops that depicts
a monk prostrate before "the image of the crucified Saviour" that has
been transformed into "the image of a voluptuous, naked woman." It
is really the secret force at work in the conflict between sexual desire
and repression that, for Freud, recurs eternally. All the interest lies in
the dynamic by which "the repressed in its recurrence emerges from
the repressing force itself," which means, in other words, that the repressed desire, once triggered or reactivated, begins to appropriate
to itself the repressing force that had been used to keep it from consciousness, just as the prostrate monk struggles to repress his sexual

desire for the woman with the repressing force of Christ, which itself becomes "the carrier" of the repressed image.

All of the central elements in Freud's thinking appear in "Delusion and Dream," but in a strangely disarticulated way. Carl Jung had brought the novel to Freud's attention, and the tactical objectives of publicizing the advances and benefits of psychoanalysis perhaps obviated Freud's closer consideration of the implications of both Jensen's text and his own, which, as we have seen, inadvertently inscribes itself into the secret history of eternal recurrence. As with most European intellectuals, however, Freud's suspicions about the ultimate survival of human beings, and about the ability of the life instincts to sustain the struggle with the ego's sadistic trends, had deepened after World War I. Perhaps despite itself, "Delusion and Dream" is about an eternal instinctual struggle, which rather takes for granted that the life instincts would ultimately prevail. By the time of *Beyond the Pleasure Principle* (1920), however, the secret alliance between Nietzsche and psychoanalysis was over, and Freud speculated, in broadly Schopenhauerian terms, on the nirvanalike possibility that organic life itself, with its carefully restricted expenditures of pleasure and unpleasure, is finally oriented, in some profoundly teleological way, to expend itself, to exhaust or discharge all pleasurable tensions, to finish with all unpleasurable and even sadistic withholdings of discharge, in a generalized and total extinction. Freud theorizes that the dialectics of *Lust/Unlust* will finally end because the entire system is seized by a still larger compulsion to spend itself utterly and totally, without reserve, without holding anything back for a future investment. And all of this would have stemmed from that very principle we saw at work in the appropriation of the repressing force by the repressed material, where what lasts eternally would presumably be this calculated expenditure of repressed desire. Freud's final theory takes one last look at the biological and psychoanalytic evidence and concludes that the death drive intervenes in the total system like a necessary and enabling principle that allows the system to consume itself. The early Freud had assumed that this reversal of energy from one instinctual field to the other, from pleasure to unpleasure (or counterpleasure), was really endless. The late Freud wonders whether the pleasure of circumventing and appropriating the forces of repression draws on a reservoir that endures eternally. "We have unwittingly steered our course," Freud writes, "into the harbour of Schopenhauer's philosophy. For him death is the 'true result and to that extent the purpose of life,' while the sexual instinct is the embodiment of the will to live" (*SE* 18:50). We might say that Freud's transition from his first to his second theory of drives represents a movement away from Schelling and Nietzsche and toward Schopenhauer.

From the question of how World War I and some difficulties with analytic therapy persuaded Freud that human life and perhaps even life in general were accidents of an incredible and ill-fated rarity, I want to turn to the Marquis de Sade's *Juliette, ou les Prosperités du Vice* (1797) and to his vision there of a philosophy of eternal recurrence. I adduce Sade at this point in my secret history because his modern and very ironic cosmology of a universe of eternal punishments influenced Flaubert, Baudelaire, Dostoevsky, and probably Nietzsche and Freud as well, by reminding the moderns that a Stoic, Heraclitean, Lucretian cosmology may very well be in the grips of the most terrifying instinctual and natural forces. Freud's vision of the *Todestrieb* (death-drive) looks, on comparison, like an almost utopian scenario, in which the tremendously conflicted tension of *Lust/Unlust* could finally expend itself. Moreover, we will see this sadistic element in some of Nietzsche's reflections on the doctrine. The question of sadism is nothing new, since we have seen it in connection with eternal return from at least the time of Parmenides. Sade's great themes of the prosperity of vice and the misfortunes of virtue (which is the subtitle of *Justine*) derive from his materialist cosmology, where Being is infinitely indifferent to life and to all becoming. Sade's idea that any vision of eternal life must also necessarily be one of eternal horror and meaninglessness captures perfectly the tone of some of Nietzsche's most troubled musings. Sade makes us wonder whether what might appear as an affirmation of life is really its tortured expenditure, and that what might appear cruel does so only in order to be kind.

Juliette's mentor, Saint-Fond, tells his protégé that Evil "is an eternal being" (*un être éternel*) who "existed before the world; it constituted the monstrous, the execrable being who was able to fashion such a hideous world":

[Evil] will hence exist after the creatures which people this world; it is unto *evil* they will all enter again [*rentreront*], in order to re-create others perhaps more wicked yet, and that is why they say all is degraded [*se dégrade*], all is corrupted in old age; that stems only from the perpetual re-entry and emergence [*de la rentrée et de la sortie perpetuelle*] of wicked elements into and out of *maleficent molecules* [molécules malfaisantes]. (Sade, *Juliette*, Engl. 400; Fr. 387)

The immoral imperative of the Sadean libertine is to maximize evil and disorder so as to be more "in harmony with his ineluctable fate [*en s'unissant au foyer de la méchanceté*]" (Engl. 398; Fr. 385). Christian theology made the world of becoming evil, but finite, with which Saint-Fond concurs and goes Christianity one better by speculating that this molecular world of evil goes on forever, perpetually rearranging itself. Juliette is struck by the proximity of Saint-Fond's teaching to the tradition and remarks to her friend Clairwil: "I prefer the certitude of nothingness to the fear of an eternity of suffering [*j'aime mieux la certitude du néant que la crainte d'une éternité de douleurs*]" (Engl. 401; Fr. 388). The Christian eternal hypostasis of the good becomes the Sadean eternal world of evil molecules. The rigor of Saint-Fond's reversal of the Christian worldview is most evident in his phantasy of inflicting eternal punishments upon the victims of his wild perversions. "Yours will be the unspeakable delight," he tells Clairwil, "of prolonging them beyond the limits of eternity, if eternity there be [*l'on jouira du plaisir délicieux de les avoir prolongées au-delà même des bornes de l'éternité pouvait en avoir*]" (Engl. 370; Fr. 357). How precisely this would work from a cosmological point of view remains unclear, though presumably, since the entire system appears to Saint-Fond to get more evil with every "re-entry and emergence," those who are victims in one cycle will be more victimized in the next, as those who are evil now will become even more corrupt.

All of these issues are rehearsed all over again in Pope Pius VI's famous "Dissertation on Murder" in part 4 of *Juliette*, which proposes something like a synthesis of eternal return and Christian doctrine. In his long speech to Juliette, the pope proposes that a truly murderous intention would seek, not simply the infinite repetition of the victim's agony, but the elimination of the victim from the infinite time of the molecular flux itself:

> To serve [Nature] better yet, one would have to be able to prevent the regeneration resultant from the corpses we bury. Only of his first life does murder deprive the individual we smite; one would have to be able to wrest away his second, if one were to be more useful to Nature; for 'tis annihilation she seeks, by less she is not fully satisfied, it is not within our power to extend our murders to the point she desires. (Engl. 772; Fr. 9:177)

What could it mean "to wrest away" (*arracher*) one's second life, one's next *rentrée* into becoming, if not to exterminate the victim in some sort of final, atomizing sense? And this is precisely what we cannot do, which means that this pope is offering theological clarification of Saint-Fond's somewhat blasphemous idea that evil doers emulate Nature's basic drives, since the pope believes it is presumptuous of humans to think they are capable of emulating the absolute, unimaginable horrors Nature intends. The pope wants nothing more than to bring the entire cycle of becoming to an end once and for all, and so he advocates infanticide as the most perfect form of murder, although it too can scarcely be imagined on a scale grand enough to be adequate to a vision of total destruction of all becoming. Is this not the most perfect irony imaginable? We can only imagine Nietzsche's delectation of Sade, since he has, sadly, left no explicit account of it. The "annihilation" (*anéantissement*) that Nature seeks in the pope's "Dissertation" thus fully anticipates Freud's death drive, but there are also some important differences.

Of course, it could only be the pope to whom Sade would entrust his complete cosmological vision:

> Nothing is essentially born, nothing essentially perishes, all is but the action and reaction of matter; all is like the ocean billows which ever rise and fall [*les flots de la mer qui s'élèvent et s'abaissent à tout instant*], like the tides of the sea, ebbing and flowing endlessly, without there being either the

loss or the gain of a drop in the volume of the waters; all this is a perpetual flux which ever was and shall always be, and whereof we become, though we know it not, the principal agents by reason of our vices and our virtues. (Engl. 772–73; Fr. 177)

Only through the most extreme violence and will to annihilation, it would appear, does Nature manage to maintain the flux perpetually in motion. But the pope's more interesting point is surely that, because Nature is so profoundly indifferent to human existence, we are unwittingly "the principal agents" of our fate. Our freedom is a kind of secondary accidental benefit of the irreducible necessity that governs Sade's absolute cosmos. We might say that the necessity of pure accident contaminates the entire system absolutely and thereby ensures its eternal recurrence. What Derrida has remarked à propos Lucretius seems to me relevant to Sade's atomistic materialism as well, for the pope's "Dissertation" articulates what Derrida calls the "identity of non-chance and chance and of misfortune (*mé-chance*) and fortune (*la chance*)" (Derrida, "Mes Chances," 22). At the level of the general system there is an irreducible sameness to the incessant production of difference, which means that chance and necessity are only subjective perspectives on the eternal recurrence of the same differences.

7

Playing with Cinders:

From Nietzsche to Derrida

It cannot be denied that time itself, unless it be discontinuous, as we have every reason to suppose it is not, stretches on beyond those limits [of infinite past and infinite future], infinite though they be, returns into itself, and begins again. Your metaphysics must be shaped to accord with that. CHARLES SANDERS PEIRCE, "The Logic of Continuity"

"Philosophical Intelligence Office"—novel idea! But how did you come to dream that I wanted anything in your absurd line, eh? HERMAN MELVILLE, *The Confidence-Man*

Of course we are still in a fundamental sense Kantians confronting the facelessness of time's aporia, still seized by the antinomy that insists both that "an infinite time must be viewed as having elapsed in the enumeration of all co-existing things" and that "this, however, is impossible" (Kant, *Critique of Pure Reason*, 398/B456). But we are also Hegelians in perhaps an even more fundamental sense insofar as the scientific understanding of the size and motion of the universe seems to be advancing at a remarkable rate. We seem, in other words, closer than ever to being able to construct what H. Minkowski, in 1908, called a *Weltbild* or "world-image," which would be a four-dimensional structure offering "a static representation of all past and future events" (cf. Holton, "Einstein's Search for the *Weltbild*," 93, 317n). Neither Minkowski nor Einstein could have guessed the immensity of the universe which today's astronomers and cosmologists contemplate. We want to have a "static representation" of the entire scope of the cycles of motion within the absolute cosmos. Although we should not forget, or pretend we have transcended, Kant's skepticism about our prospects for ever being able to map the coordinates of the general system, there is also reason to be Hegelian. Schelling's cautious middle position, in which difference becomes "an essential relation," runs the risk of turning skepticism itself into a new metaphysics. A complex posture is necessary at this historical juncture, which I have tried to sketch in terms of a very subtle fetishism that, for the time being, affirms both our castration and our noncastration from true time. It is against this horizon that Nietzsche's speculations about the doctrine of eternal recurrence must be assessed.

Let us begin with some of Nietzsche's most characteristic musings on the possible articulation of the general system. First, here are two long excerpts from his notebooks which try to construct a world-image, the latter of which is very reminiscent of Sade:

If the world may be thought of as a certain definite quantity of force and as a certain definite number of centers of force — and every other representation remains indefinite and therefore useless — it follows that, in the great dice game of existence [*grossen Würfelspiel ihres Daseins*], it must pass through a calculable number of combinations. In infinite time, every possible combination would at some time or another be realized; more: it would be realized an infinite number of times. . . . the world as a circular movement that has already repeated itself infinitely often and plays its game *in infinitum*. (*Will to Power* § 1066)

This world: a monster of energy, without beginning, without end; a firm, iron magnitude of force that does not grow bigger or smaller, that does not expend itself but only transforms itself; . . . set in a definite space as a definite force. . . . a sea of forces flowing and rushing together, eternally changing, eternally flooding back, with tremendous years of recurrence, with an ebb and a flood of forms. . . . This, my *Dionysian* world of the eternally self-creating, the eternally self-destroying, this mystery world of the twofold voluptuous delight, my "beyond good and evil," without goal, unless the joy of the circle is itself a goal, without will, unless a ring feels good will toward itself. (*Will to Power* § 1067)

Nietzsche does not need Heidegger to be reminded that such representations are only hypotheses. Heidegger's reception of eternal recurrence is really overdetermined by his intuitive Kantianism in this regard, and his reluctance to engage in such delusory world-building, which he wishes Nietzsche had taken more seriously. Heidegger's timidity is only, however (as we will see in our next chapter), the mask for a subtle duplicity that permits him to reinscribe Nietzsche's language within his own categories. Heidegger's actual analysis of eternal return has finally little to add to Nietzsche's reminder to himself: "We know nothing of the space that belongs to the eternal flow of things [*ewigen Fluss der Dinge*] (*KSA* 9:500).

I doubt that Hannah Arendt's designation of Nietzsche's doctrine as a "thought-experiment" can really be improved on (*The Life of the Mind*, 2:166 ff.). What makes Nietzsche so difficult to grasp is his remarkable tolerance for an irreducibly antinomical experience of the world, which makes him at once incredibly cautious and incredibly daring. Of the myriad analyses of the meanings of eternal return, I am still convinced that Jean-Paul Sartre has exactly the right idea about what happened in August 1881 when, as Nietzsche says in *Ecce Homo*, "6,000 feet beyond man and time," by the Swiss lake of Silvaplana, he decided to make eternal return his central preoccupation. Sartre is right to say that this was the point Nietzsche decided *to play at believing in eternal recurrence*, or rather to try to pretend it was true, for Sartre's point is that Nietzsche's last decade is really a testament to his failure to believe in his new religion. "Nietzsche *plays* at astonishment, exaltation, joy, anguish," writes Sartre, but "all in vain," since the entire "ballet of argumentation," as Sartre calls it, will end in Nietzsche's "astonishing defeat" (*Saint Genet*, 379, 380). Although I agree with Sartre that Nietzsche found he couldn't believe in his own doctrine, I don't think what Sartre calls his "leap [into] the timeless" was therefore "in vain."

Nietzsche recognized in Dostoevsky a fellow student of the Sadean cosmology; and there is an excellent sketch of the antinomies of belief by Dostoevsky in *The Possessed* apropos of Stavrogin, in a passage Nietzsche copied in his notebook during early 1888 under the heading "The Logic of Atheism": "If he believes, he does not believe he believes. If he does not believe, he does not believe that he does not believe" (*KSA* 13:144). Before the aporetic antinomy of time, the question of belief is not quite so simple as Sartre imagines. Nietzsche probed the inner workings of the will to believe ourselves immortal in one way or another.

Writing ten years after Sartre, Gilles Deleuze in 1962 argued that Nietzsche conceived of eternal return as a reinscription at the ontological level of the Darwinian principle of natural selection and the survival of the fittest. For Deleuze this is "the great selective *thought*," which finally has nothing to do with thought and everything to do with what Deleuze calls "selective being": "for eternal return is being and being is selection" (Deleuze, *Nietzsche and Philosophy*, 68–69). Deleuze thus captures the Sadean kernel of Nietzsche's materialist cosmology: our individual will has at once everything and nothing to do with the completion of the total cycle; our freedom is absolutely determined, and our fate is to be absolutely free. In our affirmation of our absolute irrelevance to time and Being, we discover what Deleuze calls a "self-affirming becoming-active," which would make of eternal return a kind of "selective ontology" (*Nietzsche and Philosophy*, 72). And this will go on regardless whether or not we have even heard of eternal return. Belief is but a remote subjective analogy to the relentless sameness with which nature differentiates what survives from what perishes. Deleuze captures the "selective" ontological dimension in which eternal return may be said to operate. Can we imagine, asks Deleuze's Nietzsche, time and space, energy and matter, as themselves seized by the same evolutionary principle of natural selection, which, in desiring nothing so much as itself, creates and destroys itself in order to ensure the infinite repetition of its evolutionary cycles, of its own innermost workings? Eternal recurrence names the relation of time and Being insofar as it alone permits what Sarah Kofman calls (in exactly Deleuze's spirit) "the selection of the most powerful force and the elimination of all the rest" ("Nietzsche's Family Romance," 48). Eternal recurrence names the paradoxical shape of the principle of natural selection in a universe of finite matter and energy.

Pierre Klossowski works some refinements on these ideas in his *Nietzsche et le cercle vicieux* (1975), which situates Nietzsche in a "tradition of political mystification" in which "*one demystifies only in order to mystify better,*" and which includes the Sophists, Frederick II of Hohenstaufen, the Encyclopedists, Voltaire, and Sade (194). Klossowski sees Nietzsche's idea that "life itself invented the thought of recurrence" as the very essence of a "generative *remystification,*" which mobilizes "the generative force of the phantasm through the philosophical use of the simulacrum" (*Nietzsche et le cercle vicieux,* 123, 195, 205). Klossowski is somewhat more cautious than Deleuze with respect to the ontological implications of the doctrine, and thus suspects that the life-enhancing beautiful-monstrous lie of "eternal recurrence not only does not determine reality, it suspends the principle of reality itself" (156). I am perfectly happy with this formulation as long as we understand that suspending "the principle of reality" is not the same as simply ignoring or forgetting it.

Of course eternal return is antinomical: it is at once, at the level of mere doctrine, "the most extreme form of nihilism: eternal nothingness (the 'senseless')" (*KSA* 12:213), and yet also, insofar as it can be brought to the level of a work of art, eternal return is "the overwhelming counterforce [*überlegene Gegenkraft*] to the negation of life [*Verneinung des Lebens*], as the anti-christianism, anti-buddhism, anti-nihilism par excellence" (*KSA* 13:521). Or as Nietzsche remarks elsewhere, it is at once pure mechanism and pure Platonism (*The Will to Power* § 1061). "It is only after the death of religion," Nietzsche wrote in late 1880, "that the *invention of the domain of the divine* [*die Erfindung im Gottlichen*] will once again proliferate" (*KSA* 9:288). Nietzsche's prophetic new doctrine, which he believed would one day begin its long rule as "the religion of religion" (*KSA* 11:448), thus places incredible demands upon its adherents. Neither science nor theology, and yet a carefully staged parody of both at once, Nietzsche's eternal return is an effort to elude the traps of both castration and noncastration. "To use parody of the simulacrum as a weapon in the service of truth or castration would be in fact," writes Derrida, "to reconstitute religion, as a Nietzsche cult for example, in the interest of a priesthood of parody interpreters" (*Spurs,* 99). But Nietzsche's doctrine is really more like the possibility of a religion of the impossible, or a religion of the impossibility of religion: "Whoever does not believe in a circular process [*Kreislauf*] of everything, must believe in an arbitrary God—thus is my observation conditioned in opposition to all previous theisms" (*KSA* 9:561). Against all odds, one might still even venture a reading of Nietzsche not ensnared in such parodic priestcraft. And this is precisely the gambit of Derrida's Nietzschean readings of practically everything, including Nietzsche himself, or rather herself, since it is the woman in Nietzsche who neither asserts nor denies truth but "continues to play with it at a distance *as if it were a fetish*, manipulating it, even as she refuses to believe in it, to her own advantage" (*Spurs*, 77; my emphasis). The woman in Nietzsche "knows that castration *does not take place*," and she knows how to exploit the "incalculable margin between castration and non-castration" (*Spurs*, 51). What woman plays with in Nietzsche is the truth about time, and what Nietzsche emulates is her relation to the enigma of the otherness of time and Being. To embrace his/her parable about a kind of eternal life is to embrace an impossible antinomy and only the fetishlike veil of a promise: "But perhaps this is the most powerful magic of life; it is covered by a veil interwoven with gold, a veil of beautiful possibilities, sparkling with promise, resistance, bashfulness, mockery, pity, and seduction. Yes, life is a woman" (*The Gay Science* § 339).

The "rude fetishism" (*grobes Fetischwesen*) of "the basic presuppositions of the metaphysics of language" (*Twilight of the Idols* § 5) wants the thing-in-itself, while the woman in Nietzsche, the Nietzsche of eternal return, affirms the antinomy and the fetish that (un)veils it. The problem with most accounts of Nietzsche's doctrine is that they fail to recognize that the fetish-veil of contradiction is the very stuff of Nietzsche's thinking and not some illogicality that undermines either its legitimacy or its underlying reason. Readers of Nietzsche who espouse a "rude fetishism" are not likely to celebrate the contradictory nature of his utterance, and will more likely point to inconsistencies and restart the pointless debate about whether or not Nietzsche really would have wanted some of the ideas in his notes ever to be communicated to the public. My objective, however, is to unfold more completely the underlying structure of Nietzsche's articulation of his doctrine.

"Let us beware," Nietzsche cautions himself, "of teaching such a doctrine as the latest new religion [*eine plötzliche Religion*]" (*KSA* 9:503). He foresaw a long period of gestation during which the doctrine will have to be carefully tended so that it can grow into "a great tree" (*ein grosser Baum*) that will eventually shelter everyone beneath its boughs (and which I alluded to earlier in connection with Yggdrasill). His effort "*to stamp* Becoming with the character of Being" (*The Will to Power* § 617), to "imprint on *our* life the emblem of eternity" (*KSA* 9:503), is thus a very long-term project. Because it constitutes a complete reversal of the habits of thought that accrued during the Christian epoch, Nietzsche's effort to "reclaim the instant as eternity" (*KSA* 9:503) can only emerge after human beings have been taught to desire *this life* rather than that *other life* of an exhausted tradition: "My doctrine teaches: live in such a way that it makes you *desire* to relive it—you will *in any case* [*so leben dass du wünschen musst, wieder zu leben—du wirst es jedenfalls!*]" (505). But how is that desire to be produced? An appeal to pleasure will be useful: "This doctrine is easy on those who refuse to believe it; it has no hell nor does it make threats."

Nietzsche continues this line of thought in the following passage, which begins to align the question of art and form to the question of indoctrination: "Even if the circular repetition [*die Kreis-Wiederholung*] is only a probability or a possibility, even *the thought of a possibility* can shake us up and transform us, not only the experience of a definite expectation. What an effect the mere *possibility* of eternal damnation has had!" (*KSA* 9:523–24). Even so, there is still the problem of how to construct a certain *possibility* that will excite new forms of desire. All of which is made difficult by the fact that eternal return remains "an impossible hypothesis" (*eine unmögliche Annahme*) rather than a scientific theory, since the underlying empirical proof is still "undemonstrable" (*ganz unerweislich*) (523). Without a theory, we are left with the somewhat inadequate instrument of a "doctrine": "*We teach the doctrine*—it is the strongest means of *incorporating* it in ourselves [*sie uns selber einzuverleiben*]. Our art of happiness, teacher of the greatest doctrine" (9:494). We should have guessed all along: eternal recurrence was Nietzsche's strategy for his own self-development, and perhaps for his own survival. Rather than quietly assuming that it is what drove him mad, we might come to recognize that the idea of eternal return is what enabled Nietzsche to keep going as long as he did. It's his symptom, his veiled promise of eternity, his time-fetish, his version of Gradiva's alluringly lifted foot. It's also his work of art: "We desire endlessly to relive a work of art. One must live one's life so that one feels the same desire toward each of its parts. That is the capital thought [*das Hauptgedanke*]! It is only at the end that the *doctrine* of the repetition of all that has existed [*der Wiederholung alles Dagewesenen*] will be developed" (*KSA* 9:505). In some manner that is not entirely clear, Nietzsche seems to imagine an aesthetic prelude as a kind of precondition to the communication of the doctrine. This transitional period would be an epoch of aesthetic self-reinvention, in which individuals learn to derive the same intense feelings from their own self-development that they had previously experienced only in connection with works of art.

Two passages from section 109 of *The Gay Science* reveal the terms of the relation between the unaesthetic dimensions of the cosmos and the demands of the art and the doctrine of eternal return:

Let us beware of positing generally and everywhere anything as elegant as the cyclical movements of our neighboring stars; as even a glance into the Milky Way raises doubts whether there are not far coarser and more contradictory movements there, as well as stars with eternally linear paths, etc. The astral order in which we live is an exception; this order and the relative duration that depends on it have again made possible an exception of exceptions: the formation of the organic. The total character of the world, however, is in all eternity chaos—in the sense not of a lack of necessity but of a lack of order, arrangement, form, beauty, wisdom, and whatever other names there are for our aesthetic anthropomorphism. . . .

None of our aesthetic and moral judgments apply to it. Nor does it have any instinct for self-preservation or any other instinct; and it does not observe any laws either. Let us beware of saying that there are laws in nature. There are only necessities: there is nobody who commands, nobody who obeys, nobody who trepasses. Once you know that there are no purposes, you also know that there is no accident; for it is only beside a world of purposes that the word "accident" has meaning. Let us beware of saying that death is opposed to life. The living is merely a type of what is dead, and a very rare type. (*Gay Science* § 109)

It would appear that the new doctrine will also demand a new aesthetic. In a related draft version of this passage, Nietzsche speaks of this world of purposeless necessity in terms of the difference between "the eternal cyclical course" (*ewigen Kreislaufs*) and the "circular movements" of the world of becoming, which is inside the cyclical form:

Let us guard against conceiving of the *law* [*Gesetz*] of this cycle as *becoming*, according to the false analogy of circular movement *within* the ring: there was never first a chaos and then progressively a more harmonious movement that finally close, having the form of the circles of all the forces to the contrary: everything is eternal, not becoming: if there was ever a chaos of forces, the chaos was likewise eternal and was to return in each of the circles. The cyclical course is not *becoming*, it is the original law [*Urgesetz*], without exception or transgression. All becoming is at the interior of the cyclical course and of the quantity of forces; it is therefore to follow a false analogy to refer to the circular movements that become and pass away, like stars or the flux and reflux, day and night, the seasons, to characterize the eternal cyclical course. (*KSA* 9:502)

Here Nietzsche would appear to move beyond Schelling's circular and rotary cosmological figures in order to suggest that the movement from time to eternity, from circle to cycle, cannot be conceived as a movement from a lesser to a greater order of existence. All the interest appears to lie in this enigmatic difference between a circle and a cycle that can no longer be integrated into any aesthetic or rational order.

There is a strange Kantianism at the very limits of Nietzsche's thinking: still the monstrous, unimaginable, unsayable form of the cycle. Under the heading of what comes into being and passes away would thus be the totality of matter and energy in their ebb and flow within the great eternal ring. This would include "the exception of exceptions" that is organic life, which, Nietzsche remarks in a draft version of *Gay Science* § 109, is "not so much opposed to what is dead, as it is a special case" (9:499). In the "eternal metabolism of things" (*ewigen*

Wechsel der Stoffe), he continues in a notebook entry from 1881, "life is so little [*so wenig*] in comparison with the whole that all the matter in the universe must at one time or another have been converted into life, and so it will continue [*und so geht es fort*]" (9:473). "Our entire world," he concludes, "is the *cinder* [*Asche*] of innumerable living beings [*lebender Wesen*]" (499). The difference between chaos and "the forces to the contrary," which Nietzsche regards as an eternal and irreducible difference, would thus be constituted by the incessant transformation of inorganic into organic matter and back again. In effect, then, eternal recurrence is the doctrine of the sameness of this difference, and thus of a certain eternal economy in the general system's consumption of organic matter and its resulting production of cinders.

"I teach you redemption from the eternal flux," wrote Nietzsche in 1882–83; "the flux always flows back into itself again, and you always step into the same flux as the same" (*KSA* 10:205). "The eternal recurrence of the same" (*Die ewige Wiederkunft des Gleichens*) is really the eternal return of the same metabolism between organic and inorganic matter, and of the same difference between life and death.

To signal the sea-change of attitudes that will accompany the new doctrine, Nietzsche offers an ironic reversal of the famous line of the Chorus Mysticus at the end of *Faust II*: Goethe's *Alles Vergängliche ist nur ein Gleichnis* (All things transitory are merely a parable) becomes Nietzsche's *Das Unvergängliches ist nur ein Gleichnis* (The nontransitory is only a parable) (*KSA* 10:397, 419). Goethe's "eternal feminine" (*das Ewigweibliche*) could not be more unlike the Nietzschean woman who is the teacher of eternal recurrence.

Nietzsche foresaw that the work of reversing such well-established orientations about time and Being will involve both poetry and harsh discipline. It was, of course, at the end of *The Gay Science*, in section 341, that Nietzsche first announced his doctrine to the world. "*The greatest weight*," he writes, is what you will suffer when a daemon (*ein Dämon*) whispers to you that "everything unutterably small or great in your life will have to return to you, all in the same succession and sequence—even this spider and this moonlight between the trees." In

an alternate draft of this passage, Nietzsche contemplates the genealogy of moonlight and appears to unfold meanings within, not only
the reflected light of the sun but in "the ash-gray light that the moon
receives from the illumined earth":

We do not yet see our death, our ashes [*Asche*], and that fools us and makes
us believe that we are ourselves the light and the life — but this is only the
ancient earlier life in the light [*das alter frühere Leben im Lichte*]; this is only
the past human race and the former God whose light and heat still reach
us — the light needs time, and death and ashes need time! And finally we the
living, we the dispensers of light: what is our force of light [*Leuchtkraft*]?
compared to past humanity? Is it more than this ash-gray light that the
moon receives from the earth that it illuminates? (*KSA* 9:631–32)

Once again Nietzsche is concerned with the ash and cinders of time,
with the ghostly "ash-gray light" with which we illumine the moon
and which makes us think "ourselves the light and the life," when we
are only the reflections of reflections. We *are* nothing more than this
"ash-gray light," an almost invisible "force of light" that borrows its
own meager strength from ancient races and former Gods "whose
light and heat still reach us."

Of course there is a sadistic, diabolic streak in Nietzsche's ruminations about the doctrine. He imagines, for example, writing "an *evil*
book, worse than Machiavelli" (*KSA* 11:241), and of using the doctrine as a "*hammer* in the hand of the *most powerful human*" (295).
For those who cannot be reached by the uncanny poetry of eternal
return, Nietzsche imagines a terrifying fate: "One needs a doctrine
strong enough to exert a *discipline:* satisfying for the strong, paralyzing and crushing for the world-weary [*die Weltmüden*]" (69). He
imagines "ruling humanity with the goal of overcoming it. . . . Overcoming through teachings from which humanity perished. *Except for
those who can survive these teachings*" (*KSA* 10:210). And in a similar
vein: "The 'Truth,' 'Annihilation of Illusions,' even 'moral illusions' —
as the *greatest means* of *overpowering* humanity (its *self-destruction*)"
(10:513). The depth of Nietzsche's resentment of a world-order that
cannot perish too soon for him is evident in this Sadean reverie:

Who can withstand the thought of Eternal Recurrence? — Whosoever will
be destroyed by the sentence: "there is no salvation," ought to die. I want
wars in which the vital and courageous *drive out* the others — you ought to
expel them, shower them with every manner of contempt, or lock them up
in insane asylums, drive them to despair. (10:85)

From this and similar prophetic passages in *Ecce Homo* about the
coming of unimaginable "collisions of conscience," it is clear that the
strident sarcasm of Nietzsche's holy war against Judaism and Christianity rehearses all the ancient horrors of barbaric mimetism. What
I think is most important about this strain in Nietzsche's thinking is
not only the banality of its fantasies but the powerful antinomical tension it reveals at the heart of Nietzsche's experience and articulation of
his doctrine. Derrida's recent remarks about the paradoxes of Nietzschean affirmation seem highly relevant here: "threat and promise
always come together *as* the promise. This doesn't just mean that the
promise is always already threatened; it also means that the promise
is *threatening*" (Derrida, "Nietzsche and the Machine," 64). Perhaps
what most irritated Nietzsche is that he recognized that the force of his
prophetic visions and messianic promises of a new order were derived
from the very evangelism he despised; and as Derrida phrases it, Nietzsche wants to liberate the strong who have been enslaved (inadvertently it would appear) by the strength of the weak with their deviously
effective ascetic imperative ("Nietzsche and the Machine," 31–33). The
messianic promise of some future good contaminates the force of
the will and in fact constitutes its essential moment. Just as Nietzsche often seems to be jealous of woman's ability to manipulate the
veils of appearance and to tolerate, even to enjoy, the terrible thought
of an ontology of universal sameness, so too Nietzsche rails against
the idea of Christian salvation because his teaching likewise depends
on the paradoxical force of a messianic promise. Derrida's idea that
Nietzsche's doctrine of return relies on the same messianic rhetoric
on which Christianity and all liberation theologies rely recalls what
Georges Bataille, following André Gide, called "a paradox: the object
of Nietzsche's jealousy is God" (*The Accursed Share,* vols. 2–3, 375).

The violence of the force of nature was particularly present to Nietzsche during the summer of 1881 as he walked the shores of Lake Silvaplana near Surlej, above all in the so-called "Zarathustra Stone" that suddenly juts up through the earth at one point on the shoreline; "I stopped near a mightily towering pyramidal boulder," he writes in *Ecce Homo* (cf. Krell and Bates, *The Good European,* 133). That was when he decided that this ancient doctrine, which he had studied virtually throughout his entire intellectual life, was now something worthy of more than merely scholarly attention; he decided then, before this spectacle of nature's violence, to fill the promise of eternal recurrence with the same force that impelled the boulder through the surface of the earth. Given the doctrine of the universal metabolism of the cinders, even the inorganic stuff of this monstrous boulder had at one point "been converted into life." Like the "secret" that the will (*Wille*) shares with the waves (*Wellen*) in *The Gay Science* (§ 300) (their secret being of course their incessant, pounding return), there is a secret correspondence between the Surlej pyramid and the force of the will.

There is something monumental about this boulder and thus also about the kind of universal history Nietzsche is toying with. I referred earlier to Nietzsche's poetic sketch on Columbus and Yorick, and to the discovery of new worlds, past and future, in the depths of infinite time. In Nietzsche's early essay "On the Uses and Disadvantages of History for Life" (1874), he describes the conditions that would have to be satisfied in order for it to become possible once again to write "monumental history." Nietzsche's account here of "the monumentalistic conception of the past" (*die monumentalische Betrachtung der Vergangenheit*) constitutes perhaps his earliest articulation of the doctrine. I cite a rather lengthy excerpt because its detailed anticipation of so many of Nietzsche's later concerns makes it a veritable script for the drama of thought that followed the illumination of August 1881:

How much of the past would have to be overlooked if [the historical account we give of] it was to produce that mighty effect, how violently what is individual in it would have to be forced into a universal mould and all its sharp corners and hard outlines broken up in the interest of conformity! At bottom, indeed, that which was once possible could present itself as a pos-

sibility for a second time only if the Pythagoreans were right in believing
that when the constellation of the heavenly bodies is repeated on earth: so
that whenever the stars stand in a certain relation to one another a Stoic
again joins with an Epicurean to murder Caesar, and when they stand in
another relation Columbus will again discover America. Only if, when the
fifth act of the earth's drama ended [*die Erde ihr Theaterstück*], the whole
play every time begins again from the beginning, if it was certain that the
same complex of motives [*dass dieselbe Verknotung von Motiven*], the same
deus ex machina, the same catastrophe were repeated at definite intervals [*in
bestimmten Zwischenräumen wiederkehrten*], could the man of power [*der
Mächtige*] venture to desire monumental history in full icon-like *veracity*,
that is to say with every individual peculiarity depicted in precise detail: but
that will no doubt happen only when the astronomers have again become
astrologers. Until that time, monumental history will have no use for that
absolute veracity: it will always have to deal in approximations and gen-
eralities, in making what is dissimilar look similar [*wird sie das Ungleiche
annähern*]: it will always have to diminish the difference of motives and in-
stigations so as to exhibit the *effectus* monumentally, that is to say as something exemplary and worthy of imitation, at the expense of the *causae:* so
that, since it as far as possible ignores causes, one might with only slight exaggeration call it a collection of "effects in themselves," of events which will
produce an effect upon all future ages. ("On the Uses and Disadvantages of
History for Life," § 2)

All the Nietzschean idioms and leitmotifs are here: Pythagorean *metakosmesis*, Columbus's new worlds, Shakespearean drama, the cosmological recurrence of the same peculiar differences, "the man of
power," and the need for a return to an ancient, monumental conception of cosmos and history. Thus far we have considered eternal return as a doctrinal and an aesthetic experiment; now we see that there
is also a historiographic dimension to what Arendt called Nietzsche's
"thought-experiment." Although Nietzsche will relentlessly question
the aesthetic dimensions of the configuration of the general system,
it is interesting that in 1873–74 he still conceived of the emergence of
organic life on earth as a five-act, or Shakespearean, drama. What is
new here is the anticipation of the peculiar importance that Shake-

speare's *Julius Caesar* held for Nietzsche, so much so that the meaning of Shakespeare became for Nietzsche virtually synonymous with the conspiracy to kill Caesar. More important still, what matters most for Nietzsche is not simply Shakespeare the artist but Shakespeare the poet who is terribly ashamed of being a poet, and who secretly emulates the political heroism of Brutus. Unlike Schopenhauer, Nietzsche did not hold Shakespeare in particularly high regard as an artist, and during the writing of *Thus Spoke Zarathustra* he made disparaging remarks about the artistry of *Hamlet*. The focus of my concluding remarks on Nietzsche is to situate his interest in *Julius Caesar* vis-à-vis the project of reinventing monumental history.

"When I seek my highest formula for Shakespeare," writes Nietzsche in *Ecce Homo*, "I always find only this: he conceived of the type of Caesar. This sort of thing cannot be guessed: one either is it, or one is not" ("Why I Am So Clever," § 4, 246). This phrase, *meine höchste Formel*, reappears later in the text when Nietzsche writes that eternal recurrence is "the highest formula of affirmation that is at all attainable [*die höchste Formel der Bejahung, die überhaupt erreicht werden kann*]" (295). The mere repetition of the phrase is only a cipher of a more significant relation between Shakespeare and the doctrine of return. In order to reconstruct this relation we must look back to *The Gay Science* (§ 14) and to Nietzsche's idea there that what is really at work in the command to love our neighbor is "an impulse for new *possessions*" (*ein Drang nach neuem Eigentum*), or that what is really at stake in our feelings of friendship is the "craving" (*Verlangen*) for something beyond the "raging daemon" (*wüthenden Dämon*) of relentless self-appropriation: "Here and there on earth we may encounter a kind of continuation of love in which this possessive craving [*habsüchtige Verlangen*] of two people for each other gives way to a new desire and lust for possession—a *shared* higher thirst for an ideal above them. But who knows such love? Who has experienced it? Its right name is *friendship*." This peculiar "craving" of friendship anticipates at this early point in *The Gay Science* the "craving" of the book's culminating argument, which concerns, of course, eternal recurrence, and where we see, not a "raging daemon," but a "whispering *Dämon*" who speaks to us in our "innermost, most solitary solitude" (*deine einsamste Ein-*

samkeit nachschiliche) and tells us that we will have to ready ourselves for "the greatest weight": "How well disposed would you have to be to yourself and to life *to crave nothing more fervently* [*um nach Nichts mehr zu verlangen*], than this last eternal confirmation and seal [*dieser letzten ewigen Bestaäting und Besielgelung*]?" (§ 341). It would appear that *The Gay Science* is framed by a notion of friendship as a kind of self-relation, a daemonic relation as well, which is to say a relation to a voice that advocates a higher sort of craving, an inner relation that makes self-transcendence possible.

In section 98 of *The Gay Science* the link between *Julius Caesar,* friendship, and eternal recurrence becomes still clearer. Anticipating his remarks in *Ecce Homo,* Nietzsche here says that he most admires Shakespeare *"as a human being"* for having celebrated the "type of virtue" evident in the character of Brutus. *Julius Caesar* should have been called, he argues, *Brutus:* "It was to him that [Shakespeare] devoted his best tragedy—it is still called by the wrong name—to him and the most awesome quintessence of a lofty morality [*dem furchtbarsten Inbegriff hoher Moral*]." In section 14 he says that friendship has not yet been called by "its right name." And it is friendship that lies at the center of his reading of Shakespeare's play:

Independence of the soul [*Unabhängigkeit der Seele*]—that is what is at stake here. No sacrifice can be too great for that: one must be capable of sacrificing one's dearest friend for it, even if he should also be the most glorious human being, an ornament of the world, a genius without peer—if one loves freedom as the freedom of great souls and he threatens *this* kind of freedom. (§ 98)

It is impossible not to regard *this* "independence" and "freedom" as code words for eternal return. Setting all Oedipalizing and/or Wagnerian scenarios aside, Brutus's dilemma, his betrayal and butchery of "the highest type," his sacrifice of the friend for some still "higher craving," seems very much to enact Nietzsche's own inner drama in 1881, which was a kind of sacrifice of his intellectual identity as a classicist and a philologist and his abandonment of their protocols in pursuit of "the freedom of great souls." Shakespeare, writes Nietzsche, "exalts" or "raises" (*erhebt*) the "inner problem" of Brutus's "force of souls" (*seelische Kraft*) to a "monstrous degree" (*in's Ungeheure*) to show what extremity must be risked in order "to cut *this knot*." This is really an odd sort of double knot, which appears to liberate freedom from an enslaving friendship even as it expresses one's even more powerful bond, which would necessarily have to relate to one's inner sense of freedom; the sacrifice of the friend who threatens this self-relation is like the loosening of a bond that is soon tightened elsewhere in the self's love of its inner freedom.

One of the most remarkable things about Nietzsche's engagement with *Julius Caesar*, first in 1874, in 1881, and again in *Ecce Homo* (1888), is that, in neither this published work nor in his notes, does Nietzsche actually cite those lines in the play that he could only have seen as prophetic of his own drama. We might wonder whether the Epicurean and the Stoic conspirators might not have shared the same philosophy of eternal recurrence. We now know, as Nietzsche could not have known, that these lines do in fact relate to Shakespeare's ongoing questioning of time and Being:

CASSIUS.   How many ages hence
    Shall this our lofty scene be acted over,
    In states unborn, and accents yet unknown!
BRUTUS. How many times shall Caesar bleed in sport,
    That now on Pompey's basis [the foot of his statue] lies along,
    No worthier than the dust. (3.1.11–16)

The immediate context is of course the anticipation that players will endlessly want to replay this bloody sport. Cleopatra makes an only slightly less familiar reflection on the necessity that destines the great figures of history to the relatively empty charade of the stage, and, in her case, to be played by mere boys, whose simulacrumlike status is highlighted, as always in Shakespeare, by the fact that a young man is playing Cleopatra complaining about someday being played by a boy. By "states unborn" and "accents yet unknown," we understand simply countries yet unfounded speaking unknown languages. Within the language of *Julius Caesar* itself, these lines by Cassius and Brutus simply reflect on the repetition of history in art and culture. Within Shakespeare's oeuvre, however, we recognize their connection to a more pervasive questioning of the meaning of time and repetition.

Nietzsche concludes his analysis of the play by turning to Shakespeare himself and to the possibility that some "unknown dark event and adventure" in Shakespeare's "own soul" might lie behind his sympathetic depiction of Brutus's struggle for "political freedom": "Perhaps he, too, had his gloomy and his evil angel, like Brutus." Nietzsche believes Hamlet's melancholy is irrelevant compared with Brutus's dilemma. But it is with Shakespeare himself that Nietzsche is concerned and with what he thinks was Shakespeare's shame before the figure of Brutus: "Before the whole figure and virtue of Brutus, Shakespeare prostrated himself, feeling unworthy and remote." In evidence, Nietzsche adduces two occasions in the play where Shakespeare introduces poets: "Twice he brings in a poet, and twice he pours such an impatient and ultimate contempt over him that it sounds like a cry—the cry of self-contempt." Nietzsche is interested only in the second scene (4.3.123–37) where, during Brutus's military conference with Cassius and their officers in preparation for battle with Antony and the Triumvirate, a poet enters and speaks of the need for Brutus and Cassius to mend their enmity. "Love, and be friends," says the poet, "as two such men should be; / For I have seen more years, I'm sure, than ye." "How vildly [sic] does this cynic rhyme," replies Cassius, while Brutus ejects the poet and remarks, in lines that Nietzsche cites:

I'll know his humour, when he knows his time.
What should the wars do with these jiggling fools?
Companion, hence!

"This should be translated back into the soul of the poet who wrote it," Nietzsche concludes. While this poetic fool is ushered out of a military council, the earlier scene involving a poet (3.3.1–37) depicts the enraged mob as they mistakenly execute the poet Cinna whom they have mistaken for another Cinna who was one of the conspirators. Realizing their error, but in the throes of bloodlust, one of the mob screams "Tear him for his bad verses." And it is true, for example, that *Julius Caesar* was first played at just the moment the Earl of Essex and his forces returned in deep disarray from their failed campaign in Ireland in September 1599. Writers in the Essex and Southampton circles were interested in the ancient classics for advice on how to negotiate the corruption of empire. Although 1599 saw the opening of the Globe, the heightened political stakes concerning the queen's successor and the Earl of Essex's increasingly dangerous position could have sharpened Shakespeare's sense of how pathetic a thing his poetizing really was. Although his remarks on *Julius Caesar* are Nietzsche's only really thoughtful engagement with Shakespeare, they seem to me to have a keen intuitive sense.

When he returns to Shakespeare one last time in *Ecce Homo,* Nietzsche's identification with him has become complete, to the point where Nietzsche can compare the experience of reading his own works only to that of reading Shakespeare: "I know of no more heart-rending reading than Shakespeare: what must a man have suffered to have such a need of being a buffoon [*Hanswurst zu sein*]" (246). On a more positive note, he concludes, Shakespeare's "vision of the most powerful reality is not only compatible with the mightiest power for action, for monstrous action [*zu Ungeheuren der Tat*], for crime, *it even presupposes it.*" Shakespeare thus stood for Nietzsche, at the end, as an indication of the possibility of a new monumental poetic history and a new sovereign experience of time. Until they are ready for the doctrine of return, Nietzsche, with clownish melancholy irony, will give them poetry. With Shakespeare and with Zarathustra, he too could say:

And I flew, quivering, an arrow, through sun-drunken delight, away into distant futures which no dream had yet seen, into hotter souths than artists ever dreamed of, where gods in their dances are ashamed of all clothes— to speak in parables and to limp and stammer like poets; and verily, I am ashamed that I must still be poet [*und wahrlich, ich schäme mich, dass ich noch Dichter sein muss*]. (*Thus Spoke Zarathustra,* 309; "Old and New Tablets," § 2)

The shame of poetic invention is itself, of course, a somewhat ironic affectation on Nietzsche's part, and no doubt on Shakespeare's part as well. Nietzsche was perhaps most Shakespearean in his recognition of the relentless and persistent manner in which human beings insist on endowing themselves with the gift of an utterly delusory relation to the realm of highest values. In lieu of the radical and irreducible non-knowledge to which we are condemned, and which makes it in fact impossible to determine the difference between knowledge and non-knowledge, the will to power remains committed to one construction or another of the truth of the total system. It is not, in other words, a question of bringing the nihilism of Western metaphysics to an end, which Nietzsche thought was probably impossible, but rather of transforming this negative nihilism into a more positive mode once the very forces of the will, which are needed to sustain life, begin to menace the very existence of the species. Nietzsche's Zarathustran stratagem, which is the poetic invention of eternal return, is intended to reorient the human will's need to affirm its own indestructibility in a more life-affirming direction. His "new path toward the 'yes,' a Dionysian yes-saying to the world as it is; to the point of desiring its absolute eternal recurrence [absoluten Wiederkunft und Ewigkeit]" (KSA 12:455) can only be reached, however, by first bringing the negative nihilism of the idealist metaphysical tradition to a kind of completion by exposing its pretensions and absurdities. And that is where the shame of poetic invention comes in, for the thinker of eternal return must continue the game of aesthetic seduction and continue to appeal to the fatuous and self-serving expectations to which we have become accustomed. In order to make what Nietzsche calls "a clean break with 'the all' [dass All], to unlearn respect for totality," we must reappropriate for ourselves and for the world of becoming all those attributes we have previously "offered to the unknown and to totality" (12:317). The poetic parables which the thinker of eternal recurrence must pander to unsuspecting humanity will necessarily be "half destructive [and] half ironic" (353), insofar as they must at once appeal to the destructive will to possess the truth of "the all" and yet prepare the way for an ironic and more realistic affirmation of our finitude.

Heidegger's animadversions on precisely this aspect of Nietzsche's thinking are always illuminating, even if they also invariably fall slightly wide of the mark. The finer points of Nietzschean irony seem always to elude Heidegger's otherwise scrupulous attention to detail, as we can see in his essay "Nihilism and the History of Being," where he discusses Nietzsche's poem "To Goethe," which first appeared in the second edition of *The Gay Science* in 1887. In this poetic *jeu d'esprit* Nietzsche performs his characteristic inversion of Goethe's onto-theological elevation of Being over becoming where what Goethe regards as mere *Gleichnis* or semblance becomes what is really unchanging (*unvergängliche*), and where the Goethean true world is revealed as a mere poetic "conceit," which is also one of the meanings of *ein Gleichnis*. Heidegger's interest is in the poem's concluding lines where Nietzsche speaks of the Heraclitean "World-wheel" that "spins by" and "mixes 'Seems' with 'To be' / Eternally, such fooling [*Das Ewig-Närrische*] / Mixes *us* in — the melee" (cited in Heidegger, "Nihilism and the History of Being," *Nietzsche* 4:236). Here is Heidegger's commentary:

[man] is mixed by the blending power of the world-wheel "into" the whole of becoming-being.

In the metaphysical domain of the thought of will to power, as the eternal recurrence of the same, all that is left to express the determination of the relationship of man to "Being" is the following possibility:

Eternally such fooling

Mixes *us* in — the melee!

Nietzsche's metaphysics thinks the playful character of world-play in the only way it can think it: out of the unity of will to power and eternal recurrence of the same. Without a perspective on this unity, all talk about world-play remains vacuous. But for Nietzsche these are thoughtful words; as such, they belong to the language of his metaphysics. (237)

These are, to be sure, "thoughtful words," but they are also an exercise in poetic irony that forecloses at the outset any possibility of a totalizing "unity." In the English translation the word "vacuous" translates *ein leeres Wort*, literally "an empty word." Although Heidegger's meaning is well rendered by this translation, Heidegger might have attended more closely to his own language if not to Nietzsche's. If he had, he would have recognized that "an empty word" is not a bad phrase for the kind of poetic irony Nietzsche intends. But for Heidegger there is no middle ironic ground between sheer vacuous non-meaning and the conventions of metaphysics. Nietzsche's ironic language is very careful to mark the intermediate interval between the old metaphysical certainties and the still unthinkable form of the general system. As Nietzsche put it in his notebooks from early 1887, from which we cited earlier in connection with the need to abandon "the all," "*there is no all*, the great *Sensorium* or *Inventarium* or repository of force *is missing* [*Es fehlt*]" (*KSA* 12:317). Heidegger's theme in "Nihilism and the History of Being" is precisely "the default of Being" (*das Ausbleiben des Seins*), and it is in this connection that he discusses Nietzsche's poem "To Goethe." It is thus particularly striking that he should *appear* tone-deaf to Nietzsche's irony in this instance, since what he seems to ignore is the fact that Nietzsche is no less keen than he is to mark "the default of Being" in the ironic mode of his poetic saying of "the world-wheel spinning by." But, as always, Heidegger's own tone is itself far from univocal, for he also aptly remarks of Nietzsche's "world-wheel" that it "is the eternal recurrence of the same, which posits no indestructible aims, but merely 'skims goals on its way.'" All the difficulties arise from Heidegger's ultimate decision to collapse Nietzsche's resistance to metaphysical positing into its putative "unity" with the metaphysical indestructibility of the will to power. While Heidegger acknowledges that Nietzsche to some extent recognized the default of Being, he remains impervious to the ironic tone that marks the tentative character of all subsequent determinations of the meaning of Being. While Nietzsche, somewhat ashamedly, risks new Shakespearean ironies, Heidegger's hope for some more authentic experience of Being's default makes him suspicious of such "empty words."

Nietzsche's language remains metaphysical in Heidegger's estimation because it remains bound to metaphysics' perennial determination to posit "the truth of beings as certitude" (*Nietzsche* 4:238), which stems from its inability to experience "the abandonment of beings as such by Being itself" (221). As a result, the default of Being, that is, its staying away or self-refusal, is what has always gone unthought in Western philosophy, which has thus always been nihilistic in the sense of being a futile effort to overcome the default of Being, to hide it or cover it over behind a delusory determination of the meaning of Being. The positive essence of Western nihilism, the secret truth that lies concealed within all the errant names of Being, is what Heidegger elegantly calls "the non-negative occurrence of non-essence" (226). Although beings have in effect reduced the meaning of Being to their need to appear to be in possession of the truth, Heidegger wants to analyze the secret history of Being that lies concealed within the history of metaphysical nihilism: "The essence of nihilism in the history of Being takes place as the history of the secret" (233). Perhaps the most profound underlying difference between Nietzsche and Heidegger can be glimpsed in their very different expectations concerning the capacity of human beings to experience the default of Being. Heidegger's thought of the *Ereignis* is his rather utopian hope that such a turn of the essence of the human toward the default might one day take place, while Nietzsche's doctrine of return is expressive of his somewhat dismissive and ironic attitude toward the possibility that such a turning could ever occur. Both thinkers recognized the underlying history of the secret and the possibility of an epoch of positive nihilism, but while for Nietzsche such a prospect remained remote and phantomlike, Heidegger, although not without his Nietzschean-Hamletian misgivings about the future, was somewhat more hopeful about the human capacity to experience "the deepening dark [that] entrenches and conceals the lack of God." We might say that while Nietzsche, despite his ironic poetic inventions, concluded that we will never be able to handle the truth, Heidegger still harbored the faint hope that somehow we might someday be eased toward it.

In Heidegger's idiom, we stand "on the edge of the time-span of undecidedness in the history of Being" ("Overcoming Metaphysics," 67); and what we need at this desperate juncture is less Nietzschean irony and more thoughtful reflection (*Besinnung*). His animadversions against Nietzsche's doctrine of recurrence are ultimately predicated by his reluctance "to attempt a venture with the truth [*einen Versuch machen*]" (96). While Nietzsche believed that there will probably never come a time when the will to power will not dominate human experience, Heidegger struggled to resist the inherently nihilistic "unity" of such a view of human history. A strange paradox may be emerging in which Nietzschean irony may in fact be in the service of a profound historical decision about the nature of human existence, while Heidegger's suspicious and defensive attitude toward irony may finally have been conducted in the service of an ironic suspension of any final decision on the capacities of human beings. Whether we can ever do without a mythology, regardless of how reasonable or thoughtful or ironic it might be, is finally what is at stake in Heidegger's reading of Nietzsche's doctrine. In "Nihilism and the History of Being" Heidegger asks whether thinking "belongs with Being's default" or "with Being?" (216). Although Nietzsche clearly decided on the former, and although Heidegger would clearly prefer to decide on the latter, we must attempt to remain (very much in Derrida's fashion) carefully suspended in undecidability. If Nietzsche goes too far in his wild speculations about the future prospects of the doctrine of return, then so too does Heidegger overstep himself when he argues that, despite Nietzsche's apparent concern for "life," the true essence and objective of eternal recurrence is "the unconditional rule of calculating reason [*die unbedingte Herrschaft der rechnenden Vernunft*]" ("Overcoming Metaphysics," 94). Situated as we are, "on the edges of the time-span of undecidedness in the history of Being," what we need most are perhaps more thoughtful exercises of the irony of poetic invention and philosophic reasoning.

8

Forgetting the Umbrella; or, Heidegger and Derrida on

How to Say the Same Thing Differently

We must overcome the compulsion to lay our hands on everything. We must learn that unusual and singular things [*Einziges*] will be demanded of those who are to come. HEIDEGGER, *Nietzsche*

The game produces the year or the ring of time that it annuls; it rolls up into itself, snail-like, a stairwell, or a labyrinth. It builds on the secret of a story in order to bring chance into line with necessity, that is to say, the proper name: indeed, to come into accord with the proper name. DERRIDA, *Mille e tre, cinq / Lignées*

There is a kind of consistency to the way in which Nietzsche foresaw completion of what should have been his work during the 1890s. He envisioned a four-part project concerned generally with his revolutionary revision of religion, philosophy, and morality, to be followed by something like an ancient satyr-play devoted to an ironic, poetic, and comic dramatization of the entire scope of his thinking. In this last part he would have turned to Dionysus and Ariadne as a parable of how the thinker, who is also a god lost in the labyrinth of time, is saved through his love of Ariadne, of the human, of the world of becoming. We alluded to these plans in our first chapter in connection with the Dionysian sarcophagal art that dominated the art of the Roman empire. I like to conceive of his sketches for books never written as being his own sarcophagal designs. His projected titles include: "Revaluation of All Values"; "Project of a New Way of Living"; "The Mirror";

"The Ring of Rings"; and "Noon-Eternity." In 1885, the year after publication of the first edition of *Thus Spoke Zarathustra,* he planned a four-part work entitled "Eternal Return: Zarathustra's Dances and Processions" consisting of: (1) God's Funeral Party, (2) The Great Noon, (3) Where Is the Hand for This Hammer?, and (4) We, the Makers of Wishes. There are many other titles and configurations, including the *Annulus Aeternitatas,* which might have been the fourth and final part of the "Project of a New Way of Living." The point of all this is that Nietzsche seems to have expended a bit too much time and effort planning poetic, dramatic, satiric, philosophic reflections, which, as a result, were left unwritten.

It is within this context that I suggest we reconsider his famous notebook entry: "*'Ich habe meine Regenschirm vergessen'*" ("I have forgotten my umbrella") (*KSA* 9:587). The emphasis and the quotation marks are Nietzsche's own. I alluded earlier to Nietzsche's notion that one day the doctrine of return, if properly nurtured, will become like "a great tree" under whose boughs humanity will dwell. And there is also, of course, Nietzsche's fondness for the Pan-like panic of the noontide reverie when the shape of the total system overwhelms consciousness: "There are thinkers of the morning, there are afternoon thinkers, there are nocturnal owls. Without forgetting the noblest species: the 'meridional,' the men of *Noon.* . . . There all light falls vertically" (*KSA* 14:241). The man of noon is the Dionysus/Zarathustra figure whose ministry as the teacher of eternal return marks a decisive event in human history: the teacher comes "each time at humanity's midday hour!" (*KSA* 9:498). Rather than emphasizing the oracular enigma of Nietzsche's seemingly Delphic utterance, I suggest we regard it as eminently readable and interpretable. In order to register the force of the vertical fall of the doctrine of return, one must face its full burst of light and heat. But is this possible? Can Nietzsche really bear to risk a full frontal assault of the doctrine? Might he not be trying, Hamletlike, to muster the resolve to do what has to be done, to forget his umbrella, to stand unprotected beneath the blinding sun of the Swiss Alps? He would have penned this note as though writing to himself from the future in order to remind himself that there will have come a time when he can look back and say to himself: "I have forgotten my umbrella."

Leslie Chamberlain has recently recalled Adorno's anecdote, which appears in his collection of essays *Ohne Leitbild,* concerning the practical joke that the neighborhood boys in Sils-Maria liked to play on Nietzsche by putting stones into the umbrella he carried to protect his damaged and molelike eyes (cf. Chamberlain, *Nietzsche in Turin,* 130). This prospect of taking a pummeling by stones from one's own umbrella complicates our reading of the notebook entry by introducing a difference between a literal and a metaphoric pummeling. In effect, Adorno's anecdote would imply, in our context, that having an umbrella is really not an option. It's really not possible to be secure during the panic of "humanity's midday hour." Let us take this reflection one step further: if the doctrine of return, that is, its tenets and its discursive or poetic articulation, may be regarded as distinct from the aporia of time and its still withheld essence, then the doctrine itself, in all of its forms, is really what is umbrellalike in Nietzsche's thinking. The apparent enigma of Nietzsche's umbrella is thus also the enigma of the relation of the time-fetish to the aporia of time. Like the task of organizing his diverse plans and of orchestrating the diverse rhetorical tonalities of his writing, Nietzsche's umbrella is precisely what remains forgotten in all his rememberings. There is, in other words, no way *not* to forget one's umbrella, since it is what always remains forgotten. Even if you remember your umbrella, you remember it only as something forgotten. Even if you think you took it with you, nevertheless you left it behind. The umbrella is Nietzsche's word for the trace of the most primordial difference, more primordial than the ontico-ontological difference between Being and beings; the umbrella names the trace of that which leaves no trace, the difference between time and eternity, or time and time's other, between our time and true time, and between calculable time and a more primordial temporality. The real problem is that of remembering that the umbrella remains forgotten, and not of confusing oneself into thinking that the umbrella one thinks one has is really the umbrella one thinks it is. Of course, Nietzsche's midday umbrella, forgotten or remembered, up or

down, is his way of naming the experience of time's antinomy, the antinomy of the aporia and the fetish of time.

This reading reinscribes within the more specific dynamic of Nietzsche's struggle to articulate the doctrine of eternal recurrence everything Derrida has to say about the umbrella fragment in *Spurs: The
Styles of Nietzsche*. The most insistent theme throughout this work,
and in all of Derrida's readings of Nietzsche, has been Nietzsche as
a thinker of "something else *perhaps* than a thinker of the totality
of beings" (Derrida, *Cinders*, 67). Forgetting one's umbrella is thus
Nietzsche's figure for a relation to *différance;* it is his name for the still
unthought difference between time and its other that underlies all talk
of Being and beings.

Building decisively on the readings of Deleuze and Klossowski,
Derrida's Nietzsche is more carefully calculated than theirs as a defensive maneuver vis-à-vis the Heideggerian reading. Heidegger's presentation of Nietzsche's thinking, writes Derrida, "*as* a thought about
totality . . . is one of the most insistent and most decisive themes of his
reading" (Derrida, "Interpreting Signatures [Nietzsche/Heidegger],"
15–16). The umbrella is like the Nietzschean cinder, which also, and
more elaborately, names the temporal *différance* underlying ontological difference. Derrida speaks therefore of "the paradox" of a cinder, because it is what, pace Heidegger, "thwarts all that governs the
thought or even the anticipation of totality." There is in Nietzsche,
clearly and undisputably, a thought of totality, and that is what Heidegger both praises and denounces: praises it as the return to and culmination of "the thought that pervades the whole of Western philosophy, a thought that remains concealed but is its genuine driving force.
Nietzsche thinks the thought in such a way that in his metaphysics
he reverts [*zurückkommt*] to the beginnings of Western philosophy"
(Heidegger, *Nietzsche* 1:19 [Engl.] / 1:27 [Ger.]); and denounces it as a
thought that "remains wrapped in thick clouds — not just for us, but
for Nietzsche's own thinking": "The reasons do not lie in any inability
in Nietzsche, although his various attempts to demonstrate that the
eternal recurrence of the same was the Being of all becoming led him
curiously astray. It is the matter itself which is named by the term 'the
eternal recurrence of the same' that is wrapped in a darkness from

which even Nietzsche had to shrink back in terror" (*What Is Called Thinking?*, 108). Once again we are back to the Medusalike character of eternal return (cf. Pautrat, "Nietzsche Medused"). We might recall that in the Pythagorean basilica built in the time of Claudius, mentioned earlier, there was a laughing head of Medusa looking more like a laughing sun (cf. Carcopino, *La Basilique pythagoricienne*, 305). This brings us to the heart of the matter, for Heidegger simply can't imagine looking long enough into the sun for the terror that one sees there to turn to something beautiful, like that monstrous vision of eternity we alluded to earlier in Nietzsche's Yorick-Columbus poem. That's where Derrida comes in, for he recognizes in Nietzsche the laughing, as well as the petrifying, aspect of Medusa's countenance. Heidegger in effect totalizes Nietzsche's shrinking back in terror: "the darkness of this last thought of Western metaphysics must not mislead us," Heidegger concludes, "must not prompt us to avoid it by subterfuge" (*Ansflüchte*). Derrida's reading of eternal return demonstrates that Nietzsche has not forgotten that his flight into fetish-thinking differs from and defers to the aporia of time.

David Krell has gathered Nietzsche's allusions to the Medusa-head as a figure of eternal recurrence in his notes during 1884–85: "In these months of explosive poetic creativity Nietzsche composes a large number of lyrics which he hopes to publish as a cycle of *Medusen-Hymnen*" (Krell, *Postponements*, 68). Here are the relevant notebook entries in Krell's translation (69):

(1) said everything once again (recurring like the Head of Medusa)
(2) the great thought as *Head of Medusa:* all the world's features petrify, a congealed death-throe [*ein gefrorener Todeskampf*]
(3) *The seventh solitude—finally* "The Head of Medusa" (the consolatory power [*das Tröstliche*] of eternal return shows its face for the first time).

The antinomical figure of the Medusa implies at the very least that Nietzsche's so-called "subterfuge" may have been more complex than Heidegger assumed it was. Derrida wants to preserve in Nietzsche a space for thinking the otherness of time that would elude the totalizing drift of Heidegger's interpretation.

The central issue I want to pursue in my presentation of Heidegger's reinscription of eternal recurrence is to demonstrate how deeply and pervasively indebted Heidegger was to the doctrine of return, how he relied upon its rhetorical and discursive resources; which is to say, I want to focus on those aspects of Heidegger's reception of the doctrine that implicitly, if not explicitly, make clear his own sense, however intuitive, that, despite appearances and contrary to Heidegger's own indications elsewhere, Nietzsche's "thought-experiment" was far from over.

I want to focus, above all, on Heidegger's reading of the poet Georg Trakl, which I will argue is Heidegger's most significant and most suggestive encounter with Nietzsche's thinking. First, let us rehearse briefly some of the basic protocols that orient Heidegger's thinking on the question of primordial temporality. Derrida's defense of eternal return as a more subtle form of fetishism than Heidegger gave it credit for being proceeds essentially by posing the most Heideggerian questions to the Nietzschean text in precisely those instances where Heidegger, for one reason or another, failed to pose them himself. Derrida has repeatedly demonstrated that all determinations of ontological difference are contaminated by the *différance* of a still unthought essence of primordial temporality. Although it is Heidegger who taught insistently and repeatedly that "the intrinsic possibility of transcendence is time, as primordial temporality" (*The Metaphysical Foundations of Logic,* 195), and who defined Dasein as our most intimate experience of how this primordial process of temporalization moves through the world (e.g., "Time is essentially a self-opening and expanding into a world" [210]), nevertheless Heidegger had difficulty recognizing these issues in Nietzsche's thinking; and it remains to Derrida to adduce those issues in Nietzsche that already pointed the way to Heidegger's concern with an irreducibly temporal horizon of ontological difference.

Although, as Heidegger puts it, "Being doesn't *go over to beings* but *transits, transports* something to beings" (*Identity and Difference,* 64), Nietzsche's gamble was to imagine that something of Being's primordial temporality did get through to beings; and that is precisely the delusion, argued Heidegger, with which the history of metaphysics has always been pleased to abuse itself. Of course, serious thinking cannot blithely assume that life belongs to Being in some fundamental sense, which is one of the many bones Heidegger has to pick with Nietzsche (Heidegger, *Nietzsche,* 3:122). *Différance* is the name of what remains concealed in that "something" which reaches beings; it is like the forgotten umbrella that haunts Dasein's experience of itself as the trace of an unconcealed primordial temporality. Heidegger too has names for that horizonal, ek-static, disruptive element in our experience of the presence of the present, which is neither positive nor negative. And one of his names for time is *einer wesentlichen Not,* "an essential need," which is also *lautlos,* "soundless," and "without consequence" (*folgenlos*). But it is not, for all that, nothing; on the contrary, it is "something":

> But that time-span [*die Frist*] when Being gives itself to openness can never be found in historically calculated time or with its measures. The time-span granted shows itself [*ziegt sich*] only to a reflection [*Besinnung*] which is already able to glimpse the history of Being, even if this succeeds only in the form of an essential need which soundlessly and without consequences shakes [*erschüttert*] everything true and real to the roots. ("Recollection in Metaphysics," 83)

Heidegger uses the Nietzschean language of the *Erschütterung* in order to make a very un-Nietzschean point about what would appear to be a structural impossibility of Dasein's ever taking the measure of *die Frist,* of the total configuration of spacetime. This is characteristically Heideggerian insofar as it conjoins the rhetoric of Kantian sacrifice to (what is here a rather vague) Hegelian anticipation of glimpsing, reflectively, as it were, in the mirrorlike history of Being, some indication of the shape of the absolute cosmos. The antinomical character of Heidegger's language, which insists on the paradox of an inconsequential shaking of everything to its foundations, is, I believe, the most general indication of the Nietzschean orientation of his thinking.

We might say that there is a considerable slowing-down, a certain braking, in the way Heidegger's language registers the motion of Dasein's temporalization when compared to the more agile modulations and the greater interplay of extremes in Nietzsche's writing. I mentioned Kant and Hegel, although the more profound fraternity might lie between Heidegger and Schelling, whose sense of difference as "an essential relation" seems to lie behind Heidegger's talk of the "perdurance," or *Austrag*, of the *Differenz*, which has very much to do with the duration, or "carrying out," of a decree, as in a judicial setting. Alert to the anti-Nietzschean tone of such judicious language, Heidegger thinks it necessary to distinguish his position from that of those who would "play music and dance before" what Heidegger regards, not as a face of any sort, Medusalike or otherwise, but as a fundamental facelessness that resists the impulse to forget that "the origin of the difference" remains even after "the dissolution [*Auflösung*] of the 'is' in the positing of the Will to Power with Nietzsche" (*Identity and Difference*, 72–73). Heidegger is reminding us, in effect, that the umbrella is still forgotten.

The main focus of Heidegger's effort to reinvent the relation of the time-fetish to time's aporia was, however, on the fundamental "unity" of the "time-character" (*Zeit-charakter*) of "the mutual giving to one another [*dem Sich-einander-Reichen*] of future, past, and present, that is, to their proper unity [*ihrer eigenen Einheit*]" (*Of Time and Being*, 12 [trans. modified] / Heidegger, *Zur Sache des Denkens*, 12). The "mutual reaching out and opening up of future, past, and present" (14) is what Heidegger calls "the four-dimensional realm" of "true time": "The giving in 'It gives time' [*Es gibt Zeit*] proved to be an extending, opening up of the four-dimensional time" (16, 17). Heidegger situates the "interplay" (*Zuspiel*) of the four dimensions of time (i.e., past, present, future, and "their belonging-together" [*ihr Zusammengehören*]), "in the very heart of time" (*im Eigenen der Zeit*). And in place of Nietzschean recurrence Heidegger endows the word *Ereignis* with the singular task of naming the singular propriety of time's hidden essence. Whether that essence is singularly finite, or the eternal repetition of the same, or something that simply surpasses thinking, all Heidegger knows is that, for now, its name is *Ereignis,* the name of the event of whatever is proper to this emergence of the world, whatever that happens to be. *Ereignis* simply names the "delivering-over" (*Übereignen*) of time to Being and of Being to time without wishing to hazard a (Nietzschean) guess as to what might be happening in the event that is happening. The mere fact, however, of the somewhat Hegelian resonance of Heidegger's emphasis on the *Einheit* of true time's four-dimensionality gives a subtle Nietzschean inflection to Heidegger's effort to push toward the limit of the aporia of time. The fetish-character of such "unity" is evident.

In *Being and Time* (1927) Heidegger already spoke of the "unveiling" of Dasein "in its being-delivered-over to the there" (*in seinem Überantwortetsein*), and of the "delivering-over of Dasein's facticity to the there" (§ 29; 174 Engl. / 135 Ger.). Because "world-time [*Weltzeit*] gets levelled off and covered up by the way time is ordinarily understood" (§ 81; 474 Engl. / 422 Ger.), Heidegger sought "to unveil temporality as that which primordially makes such existence possible. 'Spirit' does not fall *into* time; but factical existence 'falls' as falling *from* primordial, authentic temporality" (§ 82; 486 Engl. / 436 Ger.). I alluded to this passage earlier (in conjunction with Žižek and Schelling), as characteristic of Heidegger's still metaphysical understanding of "authentic temporality" as a kind of eternity, or at least as some higher modality of existence that would establish the superiority of "world-time" to the time of human history. That precisely the opposite may just as well be the case is the terrible, horrifying suspicion that Schelling says "drives man out from the center." And Schelling and Nietzsche certainly had this effect upon Heidegger. We might say, however, that Heidegger could never really bring himself to the Nietzschean point of being able to affirm such a world. To be sure, he discussed and analyzed and even poetized such a world, but despite all of that, he still resisted affirming it. Because so much more than the present is brought to presence in the "now," and because the meaning of presence has always been thought on the basis of the "now," Heidegger seems always to have silently assumed, or even presupposed, that this uncanny missing element would somehow necessarily have a profound correspondence to human being, which is to say some sort of positive relation, or that at the very least it would be the bearer of some essential values. "Not every presencing [*Anwesen*] is necessarily the present [*Gegenwart*]. A curious matter [*eine seltsame Sache*]" (*Of Time and Being*, 12); but it is one whose oddity, whose uncanniness, Heidegger is keen to contain and defuse. There would thus be a strangely inverted relation between Nietzsche and Heidegger: for while the former speculated that we would have to invent positive and aesthetic fetishes in order to cover the sheer horror at the heart of time and Being and to reinforce the will to live, Heidegger advocated trying to face the facelessness, but also continued quietly assuming that the essence of the human somehow belonged to Being, or that it was the abode of Being, while nevertheless insisting that this could be so only by virtue of a gap, lack, or default in Being. Heidegger's irony may be more complex than it appears.

As a prelude to our reading of Heidegger on Trakl, consider this passage from the roughly contemporaneous seminar, *The Principle of Reason* (1955), where Heidegger remarks that "the historically diverse names for Being and reason" only appear to be "fragmented into a chaotic dissemination" (*Zerstreuung*), and only seem "like a chaotic manifold of representations" (*eine wirre Mannigfaltigkeit von Vorstellungen*), when in fact they constitute "a solid constancy" (*eine gediegene Stetigkeit*) (*The Principle of Reason*, 90–91 / *Der Satz vom Grund*, 153). The very Hegelian expectation that the history of Being, once it is known and fathomed, will possess an underlying *Einheit* or unity begins to look more and more like a very subtle irony when we reflect that, from the vantage point of the aporetic default of Being (*Ausbleiben des Seins*), where we are now, such unity is a mere figure of speech, a promise. Heidegger's very peculiar tonality enables him to speak hauntingly of the enigma of primoridal temporality while at the same time appearing to resist the suspicion that this primordial mode of existence might be radically inauthentic and problematic. His 1962 seminar *Of Time and Being* is typical, for while at the start Heidegger appears to find "the vast reach of presencing" something "oppressive" and "uncanny," the seminar continues, as we have just seen, by construing an elaborate meshwork of "belonging-together" that seems a less oppressive abode for human beings: "The vast reach of presencing [*das Weitreichende des Answesens*] shows itself [*zeigt sich*] most oppressively when we consider that absence [*Abwesen*], too, indeed absence most particularly, remains determined by a presencing which at times reaches uncanny proportions [*ins Unheimliche gesteigertes*]" (*Of Time and Being*, 7). We might say that Derrida, who cited this passage as the epigraph to his essay "*Ousia* and *Gramme*," has refocused attention on the irreducible Nietzschean uncanniness that Heidegger so brilliantly manipulated. Heidegger's irony employs promise and threat very much in Nietzsche's mode, although in a very different tone. Remember it was Heidegger who wrote that "the most durable and unfailing touchstone of genuineness and forcefulness of thought in a philosopher is the question as to whether or not he or she experiences in a direct and fundamental manner the nearness of the nothing in the Being of beings" (*Nietzsche* 2:195 [Engl.]).

What is at stake in "Language in the Poem" (*Die Sprache im Gedicht*) (1953) is Heidegger's effort to delineate the "situation" (*Eröterung*) of Trakl's poetry, and this leads him to understand both that Trakl's fundamental poetic saying concerns eternal recurrence and that this saying of the doctrine is somehow more authentic than that of Nietzsche himself. The rhetorical center of Heidegger's essay works to situate the location (*Ortschaft*) of Trakl's poetic site (*Ort*), not in the realm of Christian theology (and it is precisely against a Christian appropriation of Trakl that Heidegger seems to be orienting, though not stridently), but in a new kind of place that is really a new kind of time; but what else could this other time be than that of the infinite time of eternal recurrence, and where other than eternal return would one speak of the poetic promise "for a coming resurrection of mankind out of earliness [*ein kommendes Auferstehen des Menschenschlages aus der Frühe*]" (Heidegger, "Language in the Poem," 185 / "Die Sprache im Gedicht," 66–67). This is precisely the "earliness" (*Frühe*) in which lies the much-treasured and sought after "nothing" of primordial temporality; and this is the path the stranger's soul takes as it makes its way forward into the vast, uncanny reaches of presencing that Trakl calls "apartness" (*Abgeschiedenheit*).

What Trakl's poetry traces is the Zarathustralike ring that passes through the gateway of the moment, which reveals that the arrow of time moves in a circle, in an immense ring that joins even the remote "icy wave" of an apparent eternity through which the stranger's soul must pass as it makes its way back around and into the "earliness." Heidegger does not, however, identify Trakl's obvious debt to Nietzsche's cosmology but appears content to point simply to the irrelevance here of the Christian eternity (194/76). His rhetorical assimilation of Nietzsche is much more studied and it brilliantly follows Trakl's unerring lead. In one of the most notable passages in the essay, Heidegger evokes both the strange earliness of Trakl's poetic site and the "rising world-year" (*steigenden Weltjahres*) that defines nothing less than a four-dimensional world-image, a conceptual map of the *Ereignis* as the shape of a continuous event:

The land into which the early dead goes down [*untergeht*] is the land of this evening. The location of the site that gathers Trakl's work into itself is the concealed essence of apartness, and is called "Evening Land," the Occident. This land is older, which is to say, earlier and therefore more promising [*versprechender*] than the Platonic-Christian land, or indeed than a land conceived in terms of the European West. For apartness is the "first beginning" [*Anbeginn*] of a rising world-year, not the abyss of decay. (194/77).

Nietzsche recognized that the doctrine of return could only make the promise of eternity credible if it could turn it into a work of art. Trakl knew as well as Nietzsche that the beautiful lies of poetry are worth more than the truth, which means only insofar as they become the truth. Trakl's "true time" is the horizon of another "inception" (*Anbeginn*) of time, the coming back of everything that was "toward everything that is becoming" (*auf alles Werdende*). What is remarkable is that Heidegger seems effortlessly to adapt himself to Trakl's poetic articulation of the doctrine, while he bristles and assumes a superior tone when Nietzsche is unpacking it.

Take the example of the phrase "a rising world-year," which happens to be Heidegger's own coinage, not Trakl's. The relation of this phrase to both Trakl's poetic vision and the undertow of Heidegger's essay makes it something of a red thread in what is to follow. Heidegger's readiness to invent, as it were, along with Trakl is in marked contrast to his determination to go against the grain of Nietzsche's language. Heidegger had, after all, shown a penchant for the expression *Weltzeit* in *Being and Time* and was thus very likely to follow up on a very revealing usage by Trakl and invent the *Weltjahr*. Trakl speaks, for example, of "the time of ghostly years" (*die Zeit der geistlichen Jahre*), or "the year of [the stranger's] soul." Heidegger cites these phrases, but he never cites the expression by Trakl that lies at the source of the *Weltjahr*. Although he insists that "earliness preserves the original nature of time — a nature so far still veiled," he nevertheless claims to understand what it is that enables the past to make its way into the presence of the present; moreover, he seems fully to share Trakl's poetic knowledge that it is the principle of pain, of unpleasure and suffering, which alone ensures "the advent" (*Ankunft*) that gathers all that is becoming into "its essential being" (182/63). Paraphrasing Trakl, Heidegger writes: "The spirit which bears the gift of the 'great soul' is pain; pain is the animator" (*das Beseelende*) (181/62).

As he had already done in his reading of Trakl's "Eine Winterabend" in "Language" (1950), Heidegger in "Language in the Poem" turns once again to the Medusa-related image of the stone as the image of the extremity of pain that the poet must endure in order to think the "advent" of true time:

And softly touches you an ancient stone. [Trakl]
Pain conceals itself in the stone, the petrifying pain that delivers itself into the occlusion of the rock [*in dass Verschlossene des Gesteins*] in whose appearance there shines forth its ancient origin out of the silent glow of the first dawn — the earliest dawn which, as the prior beginning [*als vorausgehender Anbeginn*], is coming toward everything that is becoming, and brings it to the advent, never to be overtaken, of its essential being. (182/63).

Trakl's German reads: *Und leise rührt dich an ein alter Stein,* and Heidegger notes particularly that in Trakl the word *leise*, "softly," "always leads us [*gleiten*] in like fashion to the essential relations." This line comes from a poem entitled "An Mauern hin" ("Along Walls"), which Heidegger does not cite further. If he had cited more of it, then, I suggest, he would have risked exposing his secret agenda in this essay, which was to appropriate the rhetorical and poetic resources of eternal recurrence and thereby surpass Nietzsche's articulation of the doctrine, perhaps by quietly attaching himself to Trakl's formulations, or by even more quietly transforming them.

Trakl wrote "An Mauern hin" in Salzburg sometime between February 8 and April 1, 1913. This is the first of three stanzas:

Es geht ein alter Weg entlang
An wilden Gärten und einsamen Mauern
Tausend jährige Eiben schauern
Im steigenden fallenden Windgesang.
(Trakl, *Dichtungen und Briefe*, 1:140)

[There is an ancient path along
The savage gardens and lonely walls.
Thousand-year-old yew trees shudder,
In the rising falling windsong.]

All the significant differences between Nietzsche and Heidegger are folded into this wonderfully Heraclitean usage by Trakl: the *steigenden fallenden Windgesang*, the rising falling windsong. Look what Heidegger does with it: only the "*rising* World-year" for Heidegger, who prefers here not to speak of a falling off; and what a difference between *Windgesang* and *Weltjahr*, where once again we see a trace of the seemingly eternal struggle between Heraclitus and Parmenides. The poem concludes with these lines:

Unendliche Liebe gibt das Geleite.
Leis ergrünt das harte Gestein.

[Unending love goes ahead as guide,
Softly greens the hardened stone.]

Heidegger's intuitive sense that Trakl uses the word *leise* in speaking of the most fundamental relations seems quite interestingly confirmed by Walter Skeat's etymology of *Leis* in his "List of Indogermanic Roots":

LEIS, to trace, follow a trace. *Latin. lir-a* (for *liz-a*), a trace, furrow, *de-lir-are*, to leave the furrow, become mad; *Goth. lais* (I have followed up the trace), I know, *lais,* a trace, a track, *Anglo-Saxon. laer-an,* to teach, *leor-nian,* to learn, *lar,* lore. Examples. *delirious; last* (2), *last* (3), *lore, learn.* (*An Etymological Dictionary of the English Language,* 755)

In the case of Trakl, *leis* is the trace of the umbrellalike *différance* that unfolds in the forgotten difference between the fetish of time and its aporia; it truly is a guide to Trakl's "windsong" of time. Trakl's phrase for the soft motion of time through language in "Winternacht" seems appropriate here: "The ear follows the steps of the stars in the ice a long while [*Das Ohr folgt lange den Pfaden der Sterne im Eis*]" (*Dichtungen und Briefe* 1:258). This is the softness of the soundless, the trace of time: *Der grune Somer ist so leise / Geworden,* "the green summer is so *softly* / Becoming" ("Sommerniege" / "Summer's Decline"). While Heidegger leads everything back to a gathering into some still undefined realm of essence and unity, Trakl simply follows the time-trace that rings with eerie softness in the poet's language.

But it is with the question of rebirth and resurrection that we began this reading of Heidegger's essay, and it is to that question that he returns in the closing paragraphs, which speak of the capacity of "apartness" to "carry the essential nature of mortality back to its stiller childhood." Does this not mean the imprinting of each generation with the same stamp (*Schlag*) as before? And is that not why Trakl speaks of "ein *Geschlecht,*" *one* generation? Heidegger insists that we cannot decide, since "*Geschlecht* here retains the full manifold meaning: it names the historical generation of man, mankind as distinct [*im Unterschied*] from all other living beings (plants and animals). Next, the word *Geschlecht* names the races, tribes, clans, and families of mankind. At the same time, the word always refers to the twofoldness [*die Zweifalt*] of the sexes" (195/78). No resolution of these issues is possible, Heidegger insists, and thus "all formulas are dangerous" (197/81). Rather than pointing to the obvious relation of Trakl's mythic sayings to the eternal return of the same, and rather than relating Trakl's dilemma to a certain need or longing for the impossible idea that the lost stranger who has departed into earliness will return with all the other generations in what is finally only *one* generation, Heidegger simply passes over these issues in silence. Of course the reason why Heidegger does not simply say it outright is that, if he were to do so, all the quiet rhetorical inflections and manipulations of his essay would become obvious. It is not that Heidegger lacked interest in the subtle fetishism of Nietzsche's doctrine, or that he couldn't follow its finest ironies, but rather that he chose to reinscribe them in a different tone. Rather than confront Trakl's Nietzscheanism vis-à-vis resurrection and life ever-

lasting, Heidegger turns instead to ruminations about Trakl's ambivalent position between "dreamy romanticism" and "clear knowledge,"
and to a certain exhaustion in our experience of the future, which
constitutes, he believes, our fundamental relation to time, and which
has left us without hope and struggling with confused pseudo-ideas,
presumably like Trakl in the wake of Nietzschean recurrence; even
though Heidegger will not even say this much. But wasn't that precisely Nietzsche's point, that during the epoch of what Heidegger here
calls our being without "the advent of a destiny," eternal recurrence,
with its strange mix of science and theology, will determine thinking
and poetry in the long period between the collapse of Platonism-
Christianity and the mapping of the absolute cosmos.

Heidegger noted the absence in Trakl of "the confident hope of
Christian redemption": "Why is eternity called there [in Trakl] 'the
icy wave'? Is this Christian thinking? It is not even Christian despair"
(194/76). In an essay that sets out to plot a particular poetic site, it is
more than curious that Heidegger should be content simply to characterize it in relatively imprecise terms as occupying, not a Nietzschean
topology, but only a non-Christian sense of time cast in terms of the
imprint of *one* Geschlecht. Derrida has sharpened our sense of what is
at stake in the idea of *Geschlecht* in "Language in the Poem" by revealing the role this word plays in Heidegger's 1928 lectures, *The Metaphysical Foundations of Logic* (cf. Derrida, "Geschlecht" and "Heidegger's Hand"). Derrida's reading of Dasein's *Geschlecht* concerns not
the connection to the still unthinkable horizon of "true time," not the
replication of Dasein through cycles of recurrence, but the more immediate relation of Dasein's mode of being to sexual difference; and
more precisely, it concerns Heidegger's decision to characterize Dasein's sexuality as a "neutral" avoidance of sexual difference, which is
thereby at once averted and yet preserved and postponed in its very
conventional (and inevitable) twofold form. Derrida sketches a kind
of genealogy in Heidegger's use of *Geschlecht* that traces a certain de-
veloping complexity from *Sein und Zeit* and the 1928 lectures with
their merely twofold character of sexual difference to a "polysemic
richness" in the *Geschlecht* of "Language in the Poem." The ambiva-

lence of Dasein's "neutrality" does not mean, Derrida reminds us, "that its being is deprived of sex. On the contrary: here one must think of predifferential, or rather a predual, sexuality" ("Geschlecht," 72). In relation to the thought of return, Heidegger's sense of Dasein's neutral sexuality would thus mark an important refinement in his thinking about the temporality of the Dasein that lingers on the margins and in the depths of consciousness and subjectivity. But as we have seen, even in "Language in the Poem," although Heidegger diversifies the meanings of *Geschlecht* to include family, tribe, and race, he remains just as determined as ever to resist thinking the possibility that *ein Geschlecht* might be what it very clearly is: Trakl's ironic poetic meditation on the possibility of eternal return, albeit as only *one* possibility among others. The diversity of Dasein's *Geschlecht* reaches deep into the uncanny, even though it must keep the thought of return strangely at bay.

In *Aporias,* which is in many respects the culmination of Derrida's encounter with Heidegger, it becomes unmistakably clear that Heideggerian Dasein is a very ironic version of the old metaphysical eternal substance that can never perish. Heidegger's most insistent idiom is that of a certain reliance on an ever-living substance, on Dasein, which is precisely not *animal rationale,* not a being whose death could be analyzed by anthropology or science. Derrida lays bare Heidegger's onto-theological positions and thus reveals that Heidegger's strictures on Nietzsche's ironic presupposition about the relation of life to Being reflect an opposition between Dasein's immortality and the world of becoming: "There is no scandal whatsoever in saying that *Dasein* remains immortal in its originary being-to-death, if by 'immortal' one understands 'without end.' . . . as *Dasein,* I am, if not immortal, then at least imperishable: I never end, I know that I will not come to an end" (*Aporias,* 39–40). While metaphysics reduces the temporal origins of human subjectivity to a reified form of consciousness, even Dasein's aporetic experience of time, for all its ironies, remains inhospitable to the irony of return.

The notion I find most interesting in *Aporias* is what Derrida calls an attitude of "hospitality toward the event," at once a waiting and a readiness to receive the other when he or she arrives: "One does not expect the event of whatever, of whoever comes, arrives, and crosses the threshold—the immigrant, the emigrant, the guest, or the stranger" (33). Hospitality is more than simply waiting, and yet it is not yet expectation; it is a new hybrid of passivity and agency. The idea of hospitality is also a way of posing the question of the politics of the diverse names for Being: Do they take seriously their own ontological status and actually believe their imagined relation to Being is real? Or do they ironize about the enigma within the presence of the present? Defining something like "the political in its essence," Derrida suggests it would include, at least, "a topolitology of the sepulcher" (i.e., a political topology), "an anamnesic and thematic relation to the spirit as ghost [*revenant*]," and "an open hospitality to the guest as *ghost*" (*Aporias,* 61). Are these not the impossible politics of eternal return? Hospitality is hospitable even to the doctrine of return; it is willing to entertain even this ghostly idea that the dead might really not be dead.

Of eternal return Derrida has remarked that it is "untimely, différant, and anachronic," and that it "affirms the return, the recommencement, and a certain reproduction that protects that which comes back" (*Otobiographies: L'Enseignement de Nietzsche et la politique du nom propre,* 74). This Heraclitean element in Nietzsche's articulation of the doctrine has proven one of the most important resources of Derrida's own style. The spectral quality of the still unmapped cosmos, which dwells in "blue apartness" in Trakl, seems in Derrida, from his early writings onward, to have a faintly Shakespearean character. Behind it lies, at least in part, what Marcellus says about his observation of the ghost in the opening scene of *Hamlet:*

Thus twice before, and jump at this dead hour,
With martial stalk hath he gone by our watch. (1.1.68–69)

"Jump" is here an adverb meaning "exactly," in the sense of "exactly at this very moment," "this dead hour," this perfectly suspended and suspensive "now," whose "nowness" Marcellus succeeds in marking twice ("jump" and "dead" being thus roughly equivalent) what in fact cannot really be marked at all. The "now" can never register all the spectral stuff that comes to the present with it. Whatever else he is, Marcellus's ghost is a figure for a strange peculiarity in the presence of the present. In a recent lecture called "The Time Is Out of Joint," Derrida remarks of this passage: "As if there were a dead time in the hour itself" ("The Time Is Out of Joint," 19). The expression "dead time" also appears in *Of Grammatology*, where Derrida writes that *archiécriture* "marks *the dead time* in the presence of the living present" (68). We should also note that Derrida's penchant for this expression may come as much from Lévinas as it does from Shakespeare, whose *Totality and Infinity* is full of Shakespearean allusions and seeks formally to designate "this dimension" of disjunctive, ruptured temporality that haunts "historical and totalized duration" precisely with the phrase "dead time" ("We propose to call this dimension dead time" — Lévinas, *Totality and Infinity*, 58). And in *Spectres of Marx* Derrida speaks of the ghost's eruptive commands: "*Violence* of the law before the law and before meaning, violence that interrupts time, disarticulates it, dislodges it, displaces it out of its natural lodging: 'out of joint'" (31). The realm of spectrality, which Derrida imagines watching us, looking "at us even before we see *it* or even before we see period" (*Spectres of Marx*, 101), *could be* of the order of eternal return, but then again it might be something entirely different. That is why Derrida emphasizes that the ghost's visor is *down* and that we therefore cannot see inside the armor: "the specter . . . makes the law there where I am blind, blind by my situation" (Derrida/Steigler, *Echographies*, 137). Derrida's sense of time's otherness deploys Shakespeare's language in the context of Nietzschean recurrence.

We might point out in this connection that Shakespeare's other notable usage of the word "jump" also comes in conjunction (or should I say disjunction?) with time. Macbeth is struggling with the idea of murdering Duncan:

> that but this blow
> Might be the be-all and the end-all—here,
> But here, upon this bank and shoal of time,
> We'd jump the life to come. (1.7.5–7)

The speech depends entirely on the word *jump*, which here means "to risk," "to put in jeopardy," which in this case means jeopardizing the life of one's soul in eternity by committing such a crime. And once

again the doubling of "here" heightens the impression of a mind trying to grasp the "now," the very instant within this act that would con-
demn us utterly. Macbeth's sense is that, on the one hand, this murder,
once done, might be behind us, but, on the other hand, here, on this
mortal side of the river of time, we might put our immortal souls at
risk. The issue of a violent disjunction, or difference, at the heart of
presencing is thus, when it comes to Shakespeare, not simply a philosophical abstraction brought in from outside the text, but a measure
of the most material elements of Shakespeare's style and language.

With Octavius Caesar in Shakespeare's *Antony and Cleopatra* (who
is speaking only of his immediate military and political objectives) we
might say, although on a far grander scale, that "Our fortune lies /
Upon this jump" (3.8.5–6); and with Derrida we might say that the
formation of any archive, including the universe itself, depends on an
anarchival drive, which is both inseparable from the logic of repetition
and, like Freud's "death drive," prior to and irreducible to the principle
of reality and the principle of pleasure (*Mal d'archive*, 25–27). What we
might call this "anarchival jump" is an event that still remains exterior
to thought and absolutely indeterminate. The radical otherness of this
jump into time and becoming resists all efforts at appropriation into
the order of the concept or *logos*, or any other mode of human expression or experience. All of Derrida's well-known names for the resistance of the otherness of the trace to the self-sameness of thought and
meaning (like *différance*, "iterability," "spectrality," *pharmakon*, etc.)
are adumbrations of the Shakespearean "jump" into the "dead time"
that joins the presence of the present to an ineluctable disjuncture. All
of Derrida's readings of philosophy, literature, and psychoanalysis return us to the trace of an unthinkable exteriority that is marked on the
inside of all of our texts and all of our histories. Like the *il y a* (there
is) of Lévinas, or the paradoxical "step/stop" (*pas*) of Maurice Blanchot, the anarchival jump into the dead time within the always absent
and exterior heart of the presence of the present is precisely what returns eternally, elusively, transgressively, within a passively neutral
topology of time and Being that is neither time nor eternity, neither
Being nor non-Being. Derrida's paleonymic history of the writing of
the trace reveals what, in his reading of Blanchot, he calls the "eternal

return of the double *pas*" (*Parages,* 53), which means the repetition of both the step toward the impossible "outside" and the step back into oblivion and non-knowledge. We might recall that it was Blanchot who called Lévinas's *il y a* "an-archic, since it eternally eludes the determination of a beginning" ("Our Clandestine Companion," 49).

Nietzsche's doctrine of return remains in Derrida's thinking in the winnowed and minimalist form of an anarchic, anarchival remainder of the unthinkable "dead time" that is endlessly repeated in all thought and in every language. Every inscription of the living being is bound to the "dead time" of the Other, to a still "atemporal temporality, to a duration that cannot be grasped" (Derrida, *The Gift of Death,* 65), but that nevertheless ensures the possibility of its repetition and reinscription. The automatic and mechanical character of the iterable structure of the trace, and the fact that it is indispensable to every aspect of the experience of the living being, enable, and in fact compel, us to regard it as the equivalent of both the Freudian "death drive," which is the primordial force of destruction, and the Nietzschean doctrine of eternal recurrence, which is the primordial and indestructible force of the living. The possibility of repetition and the certainty of death are the absolutely inseparable gifts, the double gift, that "dead time" delivers to the living being. The "jump" is double in just this sense, that it dwells at the source of the "now," in the very essence of "the instant," and that it names precisely what is most at risk, the very play or chance or ploy on which all our fortunes depend. The "jump" of "dead time" would thus name both the despair of the "death drive" and the messianic promise of eternal return, both at once, joined together to their mutual disjuncture, to what Derrida has called "a disjointed or dis-adjusted time without which there would be neither history, nor event, nor promise of justice" (*Spectres of Marx,* 170).

Bibliography

Abel, Günther. *Nietzsche: Die Dynamik der Willen zur Macht und die ewige Wiederkehr.* Berlin: Walter de Gruyter, 1984.

Ahl, Frederick. *Metaformations: Soundplay and Wordplay in Ovid and Other Classical Poets.* Ithaca, N.Y.: Cornell University Press, 1985.

Arendt, Hannah. *The Life of the Mind.* 2 vols. New York: Harcourt Brace Jovanovich, 1978.

Aristotle. *The Complete Works.* Ed. Jonathan Barnes. 2 vols. Princeton: Princeton University Press (Bollingen Series LXXI), 1984.

Axton, Marie. *The Queen's Two Bodies: Drama and the Elizabethan Succession.* London: Royal Historical Society, 1977.

Babich, Babette. *Nietzsche's Philosophy of Science: Reflecting Science on the Ground of Art and Life.* Albany: State University of New York, 1994.

Barkan, Leonard. *The Gods Made Flesh.* New Haven: Yale University Press, 1985.

Bataille, Georges. *The Accursed Share.* Vols. 2–3. Trans. Robert Hurley. New York: Zone Books, 1991.

———. *Inner Experience.* Trans. Leslie Anne Boldt. Albany: State University Press of New York, 1988.

———. *The Tears of Eros.* Trans. Peter Connor. San Francisco: City Lights, 1989.

Bate, Jonathan. *Shakespeare and Ovid.* Oxford: Clarendon Press, 1993.

Beardsworth, Richard. *Derrida and the Political.* New York: Routledge, 1996.

Benjamin, Walter. *The Origin of German Tragic Drama.* Trans. John Osborne. London: New Left Books, 1977.

Blanchot, Maurice. "Our Clandestine Companion." In *Face to Face with Lévinas,* ed. Richard A. Cohen, 41–50. Albany: State University Press of New York, 1986.

Bruhl, Adrien. *Liber Pater: Origine et expansion du culte dionysiaque à Rome et dans le monde romain.* Paris: E. de Boccard, 1953.

Burkert, Walter. *Ancient Mystery Cults.* Cambridge, Mass.: Harvard University Press, 1987.

————. *Lore and Science in Ancient Pythagoreanism.* Trans. E. L. Minar. Cambridge, Mass.: Harvard University Press, 1973.

Bynum, Caroline Walker. *The Resurrection of the Body in Western Christianity, 200–1336.* New York: Columbia University Press, 1995.

Campion, Nicholas. *The Great Year: Astrology, Millenarianism, and History in Western Tradition.* London: Arkana/Penguin, 1994.

Carcopino, Jerôme. *La Basilique pythagoricienne de la porte majeure.* Paris: L'Artisan du livre, 1944.

Carr, Donald E. *The Eternal Return.* New York: Doubleday, 1968.

Catullus. *Complete Poetry.* Trans. C. H. Sisson. New York: Viking, 1966.

Chamberlain, Leslie. *Nietzsche in Turin: The End of the Future.* London: Quartet, 1996.

Conway, Daniel. *Nietzsche's Dangerous Game: Philosophy in the Twilight of the Idols.* New York: Cambridge University Press, 1997.

Crawford, Claudia. *To Nietzsche: Dionysus, I love you! Ariadne.* Albany: State University Press of New York, 1995.

Danto, Arthur. *Nietzsche and Philosophy.* New York: Columbia University Press, 1965.

Del Caro, Adrian. "Symbolizing Philosophy: Ariadne and the Labyrinth." *Nietzsche-Studien* 17 (1988): 125–57.

Deleuze, Gilles. *Nietzsche and Philosophy.* Trans. Hugh Tomlinson. New York: Columbia University Press, 1983.

Dent, R. J. *Shakespeare's Proverbial Language.* Berkeley: University of California Press, 1981.

Derrida, Jacques. "Aphorism Countertime." Trans. Nicholas Royle. In *Acts of Literature,* ed. Derek Attridge, 414–34. New York: Routledge, 1992.

————. *Aporias.* Trans. Thomas Dutoit. Stanford: Stanford University Press, 1993.

————. "Avances." In Serge Margel, *Le Tombeau du dieu artisan,* 11–43. Paris: Minuit, 1995.

————. *Cinders/Feu la cendre.* Bilingual ed. Trans. Ned Lukacher. Lincoln: University of Nebraska Press, 1991.

————. "Foi et savoir." In *La Religion,* ed. Jacques Derrida and Gianni Vattimo, 9–86. Paris: Seuil, 1996.

————. "Geschlecht: Sexual Difference, Ontological Difference." Trans. Ruben Bevezdin. *Research in Phenomenology* 13 (1983): 65–84.

————. "Geschlecht II: Heidegger's Hand." Trans. John P. Leavey Jr. In *Deconstruction and Philosophy: The Texts of Jacques Derrida,* ed. John Sallis, 161–196. Chicago: University of Chicago Press, 1987.

————. *The Gift of Death.* Trans. David Wills. Chicago: University of Chicago Press, 1995.

————. *Given Time: 1. Counterfeit Money.* Trans. Peggy Kamuf. Chicago: University of Chicago Press, 1992.

————. *Glas.* Trans. John P. Leavey Jr. and Richard Rand. Lincoln: University of Nebraska Press, 1986.

————. "Interpreting Signatures (Nietzsche/Heidegger): Two Questions." Trans. Diane Mitchfelder and Richard E. Palmer. In *Looking After Nietzsche,* ed. Laurence A. Rickels, 1–18. Albany: State University Press of New York, 1990.

————. Interviews with Bernard Stiegler. In *Echographies de la télévision: Entretiens filmés,* ed. Bernard Stiegler. Paris: Galilée, 1996.

————. "Khôra." Trans. Ian Macleod. In *On the Name,* ed. Thomas Dutoit, 89–130. Stanford: Stanford University Press, 1995.

————. *Mal d'archive.* Paris: Galilée, 1995.

————. *Mille e tre, cinq / Lignées.* With Micaëla Henich. Paris: William Blake, 1996.

————. "My Chances / *Mes Chances:* A Rendezvous with Some Epicurean Sterophonies." Trans. Irene Harvey and Avital Ronell. In *Taking Chances: Derrida, Psychoanalysis, and Literature,* ed. Joseph H. Smith and William Kerrigan, 1–32. Baltimore: Johns Hopkins University Press, 1984.

————. "Nietzsche and the Machine." Interview with Richard Beardsworth. *Journal of Nietzsche Studies* 7 (1994): 7–66.

————. *Of Grammatology.* Trans. Gayatri Chakravorty Spivak. Baltimore: Johns Hopkins University Press, 1976.

————. *Otobiographies: L'Enseignement de Nietzsche et la politique du nom propre.* Paris: Galilée, 1984.

————. "Ousia and Gramme: Note on a Note in Being and Time." In *Margins of Philosophy,* trans. Alan Bass. Chicago: University of Chicago Press, 1982.

————. *Parages.* Paris. Galilée, 1986.

————. *The Post Card.* Trans. Alan Bass. Chicago: University of Chicago Press, 1987.

————. "Shibboleth: For Paul Celan." Trans. Joshua Wilner. In *Word Traces,* ed. Aris Fioretos, 3–74. Baltimore: Johns Hopkins University Press, 1994.

————. *Spectres of Marx.* Trans. Peggy Kamuf. New York: Routledge, 1994.

————. *Spurs: The Styles of Nietzsche.* Trans. Barbara Harlow. Chicago: University of Chicago Press, 1979.

————. "The Time Is Out of Joint." Trans. Peggy Kamuf. In *Deconstruction is/in America,* 114–38. New York: New York University Press, 1995.

————. "Ulysses Gramophone." Trans. Tina Kendall. In *Acts of Literature,* ed. Derek Attridge, 253–309. New York: Routledge, 1992.

D'Ioria, Paolo. "Cosmologie de l'éternel retour." *Nietzsche-Studien* 24 (1995): 62–123.

Eliade, Mircea. *The Myth of the Eternal Return.* Trans. Willard R. Trask. Princeton: Princeton University Press (Bollingen Series XLVI), 1971.

Empson, William. *Seven Types of Ambiguity.* New York: New Directions, 1960.

Engels, Friedrich. *Dialectics of Nature.* Trans. Clemens Dutts. New York: International, 1940.

Evans, R. J. W. "The Imperial Court in the Time of Archimboldo." In *The Archimboldo Effect: Transformations of the Face from the 16th to the 20th Century,* ed. Pontus Hulten et al., 35–54. New York: Abbeville Press, 1987.

Fackenheim, Emil L. "Schelling's Conception of Positive Philosophy." In *The God Within: Kant, Schelling, and Historicity,* ed. John Burbidge, 109–21. Toronto: University of Toronto Press, 1996.

———. "Schelling's Philosophy of Religion." In *The God Within,* 92–108.

Ferguson, Arthur B. *Clio Unbound: Perception of the Social and Cultural Past in Renaissance England.* Durham, N.C.: Duke University Press, 1979.

Festugière, A. J. "Le Sens philosophique du mot *Aion:* à propos d'Aristote, *De Caelo* I, 9." In *Etudes de philosophie grecque,* 254–71. Paris: Vrin, 1971.

Foster, Donald W. "*A Funeral Elegy:* W[illiam] S[hakespeare]'s 'Best-Speaking Witnesses.'" *PMLA* 111 (1996): 1080–104.

———. *Elegy by W.S.: A Study in Attribution.* Newark, Del.: University of Delaware Press, 1989.

Fowler, Alastair. *Time's Purpled Masquers: Stars and the Afterlife in Renaissance English Literature.* Oxford: Clarendon Press, 1996.

Fränkel, Herman. "Studies in Parmenides." In *Studies in Presocratic Philosophy: Vol. 2: Eleatics and Pluralists,* ed. R. E. Allen and David J. Furley, 1–47. Atlantic Highlands, N.J.: Humanities Press, 1975.

Freeman, Kathleen. *Ancilla to the Presocratic Philosophers.* Cambridge, Mass.: Harvard University Press, 1957.

Freud, Sigmund. *Delusion and Dream.* Ed. Philip Rieff. Boston: Beacon Press, 1956.

———. *Gesammelte Werke.* Ed. Anna Freud et al. 19 vols. Frankfurt am Main: S. Fischer Verlag, 1987.

———. *The Standard Edition of the Complete Psychological Works.* Ed. James Strachey et al. 24 vols. London: Hogarth Press, 1974. [*SE*]

Furley, David. *Cosmic Problems: Essays on Greek and Roman Philosophy of Nature.* Cambridge: Cambridge University Press, 1989.

Gorman, Peter. *Pythagoras: A Life.* London: Routledge & Kegan Paul, 1979.

Guibbory, Achsah. *The Map of Time: Seventeenth-Century English Literature and Ideas of Pattern in History.* Urbana: University of Illinois Press, 1979.

Guthrie, Kenneth Sylvan. *Numenius: The Father of Neo-Platonism.* Alpine, N.J.: Comparative Literature Press, 1917.

———. *The Pythagorean Sourcebook.* Grand Rapids, Mich.: Phanes Press, 1987.

Guy, John, ed. *The Reign of Elizabeth I: Court and Culture in the Last Decade.* Cambridge: Cambridge University Press, 1995.

Haar, Michel. *Nietzsche and Metaphysics.* Trans. Michael Gendre. Albany: State University of New York Press, 1996.

Hamacher, Werner. "Peut-être la question." In *Les Fins de l'homme: autour du travail de Jacques Derrida,* ed. Philippe Lacoue-Labarthe and Jean-Luc Nancy, 345–65. Paris: Galilée, 1981.

Havas, Randall. *Nietzsche's Genealogy: Nihilism and the Will to Knowledge.* Ithaca, N.Y.: Cornell University Press, 1995.

Heidegger, Martin. "The Anaximander Fragment." In *Early Greek Thinking,* trans. David Farrell Krell and Frank A. Capuzzi, 13–58. New York: Harper & Row, 1975.

———. *Being and Time.* Trans. John Macquarrie and Edward Robinson. New York: Harper & Row, 1962.

———. *Identity and Difference.* Trans. Joan Stambaugh. New York: Harper & Row, 1974.

———. "Kant's Thesis on Being." Trans. Ted E. Klein and William E. Pohl. In *Thinking about Being: Aspects of Heidegger's Thought,* ed. Robert W. Shahan and J. N. Mohanty, 7–34. Norman: University of Oklahoma Press, 1984.

———. "Language." In *Poetry, Language, Thought,* trans. Albert Hofstadter, 189–210. New York: Harper & Row, 1971.

———. "Language in the Poem." In *On the Way to Language,* trans. Peter D. Hertz, 159–98. New York: Harper & Row, 1971.

———. "Metaphysics as History of Being." In *The End of Philosophy,* trans. Joan Stambaugh, 1–54. New York: Harper & Row, 1973.

———. *Nietzsche.* 2 vols. Pfullingen: Neske, 1961.

———. *Nietzsche.* 4 vols. Trans. David Farrell Krell and Frank A. Capuzzi. San Francisco: Harper & Row, 1982–87.

———. "Nihilism as Determined by the History of Being." In *Nietzsche,* trans. Frank A. Capuzzi, 4:197–250.

———. *On Time and Being.* Trans. Joan Stambaugh. New York: Harper & Row, 1972.

———. "Overcoming Metaphysics." In *The End of Philosophy,* trans. Joan Stambaugh, 84–110. New York: Harper & Row, 1973.

———. *The Principle of Reason.* Trans. Reginald Lilly. Bloomington: Indiana University Press, 1991.

————. "Recollection in Metaphysics." In *The End of Philosophy*, trans. Joan Stambaugh, 75–83.

————. *Unterwegs zur Sprache*. Pfullingen: Neske: 1982.

————. *What Is Called Thinking?* Trans. J. Glenn Gray. San Francisco: Harper & Row, 1968.

————. *Zur Sache des Denkens*. Tübingen: Max Niemeyer Verlag, 1969.

Hegel, G. W. F. *Lectures on the History of Philosophy*. Trans. F. S. Haldane and Frances H. Simson. 3 vols. London: Routledge & Kegan Paul, 1968.

————. *Phenomenology of Spirit*. Trans. A. V. Miller. Oxford: Oxford University Press, 1977.

————. *Science of Logic*. Trans. A. V. Miller. New York: Humanities Press, 1976.

————. *Werke*. Ed. Eva Moldenhauer and Karl Markus. 20 vols. Frankfurt am Main: Suhrkamp, 1971.

Heninger, S. K. *The Cosmographical Glass: Renaissance Diagrams of the Universe*. San Marino, Calif.: Huntington Library, 1977.

————. *Touches of Sweet Harmony: Pythagorean Cosmology and Renaissance Poetics*. San Marino, Calif.: Huntington Library, 1974.

Henrichs, Albert. " 'He Has a God in Him': Human and Divine in the Modern Perception of Dionysus." In *Masks of Dionysus*, ed. Thomas H. Carpenter and Christopher A. Fadone, 13–43. Ithaca, N.Y.: Cornell University Press, 1993.

Hervey, Mary F. S. *Holbein's 'Ambassadors': The Picture and the Men: An Historical Study*. London: George Bell & Sons, 1900.

Hölderlin, Friedrich. "Bread and Wine." Trans. Michael Hamburger. In *Hyperion and Selected Poems*, ed. Eric Santner, 178–88. New York: Continuum, 1990.

Holton, Gerard. "Einstein's Search for the *Weltbild*." In *The Advancement of Science and Its Burdens*, 77–104. Cambridge: Cambridge University Press, 1986.

Hurstfield, Joel. *Freedom, Corruption, and Government in Elizabethan England*. Cambridge, Mass.: Harvard University Press, 1973.

Iocono, Alfonzo. *Le Fétichisme*. Paris: Presses Universitaires de France, 1992.

Irigaray, Luce. *Marine Lover of Friedrich Nietzsche*. Trans. Gillian C. Gill. New York: Columbia University Press, 1991.

Jaeger, Werner. *The Theology of the Early Greek Philosophers*. Oxford: Clarendon Press, 1960.

James, Mervyn. *Society, Politics, and Culture: Studies in Early Modern England*. Cambridge: Cambridge University Press, 1986.

Jaspers, Karl. *Nietzsche: An Introduction to the Understanding of His Philo-*

sophical Activity. Trans. Charles F. Wallraff and Frederick K. Schmitz. South Bend, Ind.: Reggnery/Gateway, 1965.

Jensen, Wilhelm. *Gradiva: A Pompeiian Fancy.* Trans. Harry Zohn. In Sigmund Freud, *Delusion and Dream,* ed. Philip Rieff, 146–235.

Jung, C. G. *Nietzsche's 'Zarathustra': Notes of the Seminar Given in 1934–1939.* Ed. James L. Jarrett. 2 vols. Princeton: Princeton University Press (Bollingen Series XCIX), 1988.

Kahn, Charles H. *The Art and Thought of Heraclitus: An Edition of the Fragments with Translation and Commentary.* Cambridge: Cambridge University Press, 1979.

Kant, Immanuel. *Critique of Pure Reason.* Trans. Norman Kemp Smith. New York: St. Martin's Press, 1967.

———. *Critique of Judgement.* Trans. J. H. Bernard. New York: Hafner, 1966.

Kantorowicz, Ernst. *The King's Two Bodies: A Study in Medieval Political Theology.* Princeton: Princeton University Press, 1958.

———. "Mysteries of State: An Absolutist Concept and Its Late Medieval Origins." In *Selected Studies,* 381–97. Locust Valley, N.Y.: J. J. Augustin, 1965.

Keats, John. *The Complete Poems.* 3rd ed. Ed. John Barnard. New York: Penguin, 1988.

Kemp, Martin. *The Science of Art: Optical Theories in Western Art from Brunelleschi to Seurat.* New Haven: Yale University Press, 1990.

Kerényi, C. *Dionysos: Archetypal Image of Indestructible Life.* Trans. Ralph Manheim. Princeton: Princeton University Press (Bollingen Series LX, vol. 2), 1976.

Kingsley, Peter. *Ancient Philosophy, Mystery, and Magic: Empedocles and Pythagorean Tradition.* Oxford: Clarendon Press, 1995.

Kirk, G. S., and J. E. Raven. *The Presocratic Philosophers: A Critical History with a Selection of Texts.* Cambridge: Cambridge University Press, 1964.

Klossowski, Pierre. *Nietzsche et le cercle vicieux.* Paris: Mercure de France, 1975.

Kofman, Sarah. "Baubô: Theological Perversion and Fetishism." Trans. Tracy B. Strong. In *Nietzsche's New Seas: Explorations in Philosophy, Aesthetics, and Politics,* ed. Michael Allen Gillepsie, 175–202. Chicago: University of Chicago Press, 1988.

———. "A Fantastical Genealogy: Nietzsche's Family Romance." In *Nietzsche and the Feminine,* ed. Peter J. Burgard, 35–52. Charlottesville: University Press of Virginia, 1994.

Krell, David Farrell. *Daimon Life: Heidegger and Life-Philosophy.* Bloomington, Ind.: Indiana University Press, 1992.

———. *Infectious Nietzsche.* Bloomington, Ind.: Indiana University Press, 1996.

———. *Nietzsche: A Novel.* Albany: State University of New York Press, 1996.

———. *Postponements: Women, Sensuality, and Death in Nietzsche.* Bloomington, Ind.: Indiana University Press, 1986.

———, and Donald Bates. *The Good European: Nietzsche's Work Sites in Word and Image.* Chicago: University of Chicago Press, 1997.

Lacan, Jacques. *The Ethics of Psychoanalysis.* Trans. Dennis Porter. New York: Norton, 1993.

———. *Four Fundamental Concepts of Psycho-Analysis.* Trans. Alan Sheridan. New York: Norton, 1978.

———. "Kant with Sade." Trans. James Swenson. *October* 51 (1990): 51–76.

Lange, Frederick Albert. *The History of Materialism: And Criticism of Its Present Importance.* Trans. Ernest Chester Thomas. 3rd ed. 3 vols. in one. Intro. Bertrand Russell. New York: Harcourt, Brace, 1925.

Lee, Sidney. "Ovid and Shakespeare's Sonnets." In *Elizabethan and Other Studies,* ed. Frederick S. Boas, 116–39. Oxford: Clarendon Press, 1929.

Lévinas, Emmanuel. *Totality and Infinity.* Trans. Alphonso Lingis. Pittsburgh: Duquesne University Press, 1969.

Löwith, Karl. *Nietzsche's Philosophy of the Eternal Recurrence of the Same.* Trans. J. Harvey Lomax. Berkeley: University of California Press, 1997.

Lukacher, Ned. *Daemonic Figures: Shakespeare and the Question of Conscience.* Ithaca, N.Y.: Cornell University Press, 1994.

Lyotard, Jean-François. *Economie libidinale.* Paris: Minuit, 1974.

Magnus, Brend. *Nietzsche's Existential Imperative.* Bloomington, Ind.: Indiana University Press, 1978.

———, with Stanley Stewart and Jean-Pierre Mileur. *Nietzsche's Case: Philosophy as/and Literature.* New York: Routledge, 1993.

Mallin, Eric. *Inscribing the Time: Shakespeare and the End of Elizabethan England.* Berkeley: University of California Press, 1995.

Mallet, Paul Henri. *Northern Antiquities.* Trans. Bishop Percy. Ed. I. A. Blackwell. London: Henry G. Bohn, 1847.

Matz, Friedrich. *Die Dionysischen Sarkophage.* 4 vols. Berlin: Gebr. Mann Verlag, 1969.

McCoy, Richard C. "Love's Martyrs: Shakespeare's 'Phoenix and Turtle' and the Sacrificial Sonnets." In *Religion and Culture in Renaissance England,* ed. Claire McEachern and Debra Shuger, 188–208. Cambridge: Cambridge University Press, 1997.

McKirahan, Richard D. *Philosophy before Socrates: An Introduction with Texts and Commentary.* Indianapolis: Hackett, 1994.

Meleager. *The Poems of Meleager.* Trans. Peter Whigham and Peter Jay. Berkeley: University of California Press, 1975.

Meres, Francis. *Palladis Tamia. Wit's Treasury, Being the Second Part of Wits Commonwealth.* London, 1598; reprint, New York: Garland, 1992.

Miller, James. *Measures of Wisdom: The Cosmic Dance in Classical and Christian Antiquity.* Toronto: University of Toronto Press, 1986.

Montaigne, Michel de. *Complete Essays.* Trans. Donald M. Frame. Stanford: Stanford University Press, 1965.

———. *Complete Essays.* Trans. M. A. Screech. New York: Allen Lane / Penguin, 1991.

———. *Essais.* Ed. Maurice Rat. 3 vols. Paris: Garnier Frères, 1958.

———. *Essays.* Trans. John Florio. 3 vols. New York: Dent/Dutton, 1965.

Mugler, Charles. *Deux thèmes de la cosmologie grecque: Devenir cyclique et pluralité des mondes.* Paris: C. Klincksieck, 1953.

Myers, K. Sara. *Ovid's Causes: Cosmogony and Aetiology in the "Metamorphoses."* Ann Arbor: University of Michigan Press, 1994.

Nancy, Jean-Luc. *The Sense of the World.* Trans. Jeffrey Librett. Minneapolis: University of Minnesota Press, 1997.

———. "De l'être singulier pluriel." In *Etre singulier pluriel,* 15–123. Paris: Galilée, 1996.

Nietzsche, Friedrich. *Dithyrambs of Dionysus.* Trans. R.J. Hollingdale. Redding Ridge, Conn.: Black Swan, 1984.

———. *Ecce Homo.* Trans. Walter Kaufmann. New York: Vintage Books, 1969.

———. *The Gay Science.* Trans. Walter Kaufmann. New York: Vintage Books, 1974.

———. *Kritische Studienausgabe.* Ed. Giorgio Colli and Mazzino Montinari. 15 vols. Munich/Berlin: DTV/Walter de Gruyter, 1988. [*KSA*]

———. "On the Uses and Disadvantages of History for Life." Trans. R. J. Hollingdale. In *Untimely Meditations,* 57–124. Cambridge: Cambridge University Press, 1983.

———. *Philosophy and Truth.* Trans. Daniel Breazeale. Atlantic Highlands, N.J.: Humanities Press, 1990.

———. *Philosophy in the Tragic Age of the Greeks.* Trans. Marianne Cowan. South Bend, Ind.: Gateway Editions, 1962.

———. *Thus Spoke Zarathustra.* Trans. Walter Kaufmann. In *The Portable Nietzsche.* New York: Viking/Penguin, 1968.

———. *Twilight of the Idols.* In *The Portable Nietzsche.* New York: Viking/ Penguin, 1968.

———. *The Will to Power.* Trans. Walter Kaufmann. New York: Random House, 1966.

Norbrook, David. "The Emperor's New Body?: *Richard II*, Ernst Kantorow-icz, and the Politics of Shakespeare Criticism." *Textual Practice* 10 (1996): 329–57.

———. "Rhetoric, Ideology, and the Elizabethan World Picture." In *Renaissance Rhetoric*, ed. Peter Mack, 140–64. London: Macmillan, 1994.

Oliver, Kelly. *Womanizing Nietzsche*. New York: Routledge, 1995.

Otis, Brooks. *Ovid as Epic Poet*. 2nd ed. Cambridge: Cambridge University Press, 1970.

Ovid. *The Art of Love, and Other Poems*. Trans. J. H. Loeb Classical Library. Cambridge, Mass.: Harvard University Press, 1962.

———. *Fasti*. Trans. and commentary by Sir James George Frazer. 5 vols. London: Macmillan, 1929.

———. *Fasti*. Trans. Sir James George Frazer. 2nd ed., rev. G. P. Goold. Loeb Classical Library. Cambridge, Mass.: Harvard University Press, 1989.

———. *Heroides and Amores*. Trans. Grant Showerman. 2nd ed., rev. G. P. Goold. Loeb Classical Library. Cambridge, Mass.: Harvard University Press, 1986.

———. *Metamorphoses*. Trans. Arthur Golding. New York: Macmillan, 1925.

———. *Metamorphoses*. Trans. Frank Justus Miller. 2nd ed., rev. G. P. Goold. 2 vols. Loeb Classical Library. Cambridge, Mass.: Harvard University Press, 1977.

———. *Metamorphoses*. Trans. A. D. Melville. Oxford: Oxford University Press, 1987.

———. *Sorrows of an Exile*. Trans. A. D. Melville. Oxford: Oxford University Press, 1995.

———. *Tristia ex Ponto*. Trans. A. L. Wheeler. 2nd ed., rev. G. P. Goold. Loeb Classical Library. Cambridge, Mass.: Harvard University Press, 1988.

Owen, G. E. L. "Aristotle on Time." In *Logic, Science and Dialectic: Collected Papers in Greek Philosophy*, ed. Martha Nussbaum, 295–314. Ithaca, N.Y.: Cornell University Press, 1986.

Panofsky, Erwin. *Problems in Titian: Mostly Iconographic*. New York: New York University Press, 1969.

Parmenides of Elea. *Fragments: A Text and Translation*. Ed. David Gallop. Toronto: University of Toronto Press, 1984.

Pautrat, Bernard. "Nietzsche Medused." Trans. Peter Connor. In *Looking After Nietzsche*, ed. Laurence A. Rickels, 159–73. Albany: State University Press of New York, 1990.

Pickard-Cambridge, Sir Arthur. *The Dramatic Festivals of Athens*. 2nd ed., rev. John Gould and D. M. Lewis. Oxford: Clarendon Press, 1968.

Plato. *Timaeus*. Trans. R. G. Bury. Loeb Classical Library. Cambridge, Mass.: Harvard University Press, 1929.

Plotinus. *The Enneads*. Trans. A. H. Armstrong. 7 vols. Loeb Classical Library. Cambridge, Mass.: Harvard University Press, 1970–92.

———. *The Enneads*. Ed. John Dillon. New York: Penguin/Viking, 1995.

———. *The Enneads*. Trans. Stephen MacKenna. 4th ed., rev. B. S. Page. London: Faber & Faber, 1969.

Puttenham, George. *The Arte of English Poesie*. [Facsimile of 1st ed., 1589] Kent, Ohio: Kent State University Press, 1988.

Rawson, Elizabeth. *Intellectual Life in the Late Roman Republic*. London: Duckworth, 1985.

Sade, Donatien Alphonse [Marquis de]. *Juliette*. Trans. Austryn Wainhouse. New York: Grove Press, 1968.

———. *Juliette*. Vols. 8–9 in *Oeuvres complètes*. 15 vols. Paris: Au Cercle du Livre Précieux, 1967.

Sadler, Ted. *Heidegger and Aristotle: The Question of Being*. London: Athlone Press, 1996.

———. *Nietzsche: Truth and Redemption, Critique of the Postmodern Nietzsche*. London: Athlone Press, 1995.

Sallis, John, and Kenneth Maly, eds. *Heraclitean Fragments: A Companion Volume to the Heidegger/Fink Seminar on Heraclitus*. University, Ala.: University of Alabama Press, 1978.

Sartre, Jean-Paul. *Saint Genet*. Trans. Bernard Frechtman. New York: NAL, 1964.

Schelling, F. W. J. von. *The Ages of the World*. Trans. Frederick de Wolfe Bolman. New York: Columbia University Press, 1942.

———. *Ages of the World*. Trans. Judith Norman. In Slavoj Žižek and F. W. J. von Schelling, *The Abyss of Freedom/Ages of the World*, 105–82. Ann Arbor: University of Michigan Press, 1997.

———. *Of Human Freedom*. Trans. James Guttman. Chicago: Open Court, 1936.

Schopenhauer, Arthur. "Essay on Spirit Seeing and Everything Connected Therewith." In *Parerga and Paralipomena*. Trans. E. F. J. Payne. 2 vols. 1:225–304. Oxford: Clarendon Press, 1974.

———. "Ideas Concerning the Intellect Generally and in All Respects." In *Parerga and Paralipomena*. 2:31–89.

———. *Manuscript Remains in Four Volumes*. Ed. Arthur Hübscher. Trans. E. F. J. Payne. Oxford/New York/Munich: Berg, 1988–90.

———. "On Judgement, Criticism, Approbation, and Fame." In *Parerga and Paralipomena*. 2:453–78.

———. "Some Observations on the Antithesis of the Thing-in-Itself and the Phenomenon." In *Parerga and Paralipomena*. 2:90–99.

———. "Transcendent Speculation on the Apparent Deliberateness in the Fate of the Individual." In *Parerga and Paralipomena*. 1:199–224.

———. *The World as Will and Representation*. Trans. E. F. J. Payne. 2 vols. Indian Hills, Colo.: Falcon Wing Press, 1958.

Schrift, Alan. *Nietzsche's French Legacy: A Genealogy of Poststructuralism*. New York: Routledge, 1995.

Schulte-Sasse, Jochen, ed. *Theory as Practice: A Critical Anthology of Early German Romantic Writing*. Minneapolis: University of Minnesota Press, 1996.

Seronsy, Cecil. "The Doctrine of Cyclical Recurrence and Some Related Ideas in the Works of Samuel Daniel." *Studies in Philology* 54 (1957): 387–407.

Shakespeare, William. *The Norton Shakespeare,* ed. Stephen Greenblatt, Walter Cohen, Jean Howard, Katharine Eisaman Maus. New York: W. W. Norton, 1997.

———. *Sonnets*. Ed. Stephen Booth. New Haven: Yale University Press, 1977.

———. *Sonnets*. Ed. John Kerrigan. New York: Penguin, 1986.

Shickman, Allan. " 'Turning Pictures' in Shakespeare's England." *Art Bulletin* 59 (1977): 67–70.

Skeat, Walter W. *An Etymological Dictionary of the English Language*. Oxford: Clarendon Press, 1910.

Sophocles. *Antigone*. In *Works*, vol. 2, ed. and trans. Hugh Lloyd-Jones, 1–127. Loeb Classical Library. Cambridge, Mass.: Harvard University Press, 1994.

Sorabji, Richard. *Time, Creation, and the Continuum: Theories in Antiquity and the Early Middle Ages*. Ithaca, N.Y.: Cornell University Press, 1983.

Spaeth, Barbette Stanley. *The Roman Goddess Ceres*. Austin: University of Texas Press, 1996.

Stack, George. *Lange and Nietzsche*. Berlin: Walter de Gruyter, 1983.

Stambaugh, Joan. *Nietzsche's Thought of Eternal Return*. Baltimore: Johns Hopkins University Press, 1972.

Strong, Roy. *Tudor and Jacobean Portraits*. London: Her Majesty's Stationery Office, 1969.

Theunissen, Michael. "Metaphysics' Fogetfulness of Time: On the Controversy over Parmenides, Frag. 8, 5." In *Philosophical Interventions in the Unfinished Project of Enlightenment*, ed. Axel Honneth, Thomas McCarthy, Claus Offe, and Albrecht Wellmer, 3–28. Cambridge, Mass.: MIT Press, 1992.

Trakl, Georg. *Dichtungen und Briefe.* Ed. Walther Killy and Hans Szklenar. 2 vols. Salzburg: Otto Müller, 1969.

Trompf, G. W. *The Idea of Historical Recurrence in Western Thought: From Antiquity to the Reformation.* Berkeley: University of California, 1979.

Turcan, Robert. *Les Sarcophages romains à représentations dionysiaques: Essai de chronologie et d'histoire réligieuse.* Paris: E. de Boccard, 1966.

Waterhouse, Ellis. *Painting in Britain 1530–1790.* London: Penguin, 1953.

Wilkinson, L. P. *Ovid Surveyed.* Cambridge: Cambridge University Press, 1962.

Winstanley, Lilian. *Hamlet and the Scottish Succession.* Cambridge: Cambridge University Press, 1921.

Wood, David. *The Deconstruction of Time.* Atlantic Highlands, N.J.: Humanities Press International, 1989.

———. "Reiterating the Temporal: Toward a Rethinking of Heidegger on Time." In *Reading Heidegger: Commemorations,* ed. John Sallis, 136–62. Bloomington: Indiana University Press, 1993.

Wright, George. "Hendiadys and Hamlet." *PMLA* 96 (1981): 166–91.

Wright, M. R. *Cosmology in Antiquity.* London: Routledge, 1995.

Žižek, Slavoj. *The Abyss of Freedom.* In Žižek and F. W. J. von Schelling, *The Abyss of Freedom / Ages of the World,* 1–104. Ann Arbor: University of Michigan Press, 1997.

Index

Ned Lukacher is Professor of English at the University of Illinois
at Chicago. He is the author of *Primal Scenes: Literature, Philosophy,
Psychoanalysis* and *Daemonic Figures: Shakespeare and the Question
of Conscience.*

Library of Congress Cataloging-in-Publication Data

Lukacher, Ned.
Time-fetishes : the secret history of eternal recurrence / Ned Lukacher.
p.   cm. — (Post-contemporary interventions)
Includes bibliographical references and index.
ISBN 0-8223-2253-6 (hardcover : alk. paper). —
ISBN 0-8223-2273-0 (pbk. : alk. paper)
1. Eternal return — History.   I. Title.   II. Series.
BD639.L85   1998
115 — dc21   98-18862